Stein[illegible]

Cats

Dear David:

Cisco helped me pick this out... I know you'll get much pleasure from this little book.

Happy 32nd

Lots of Love,

Julie ♡ + Cisco ♡

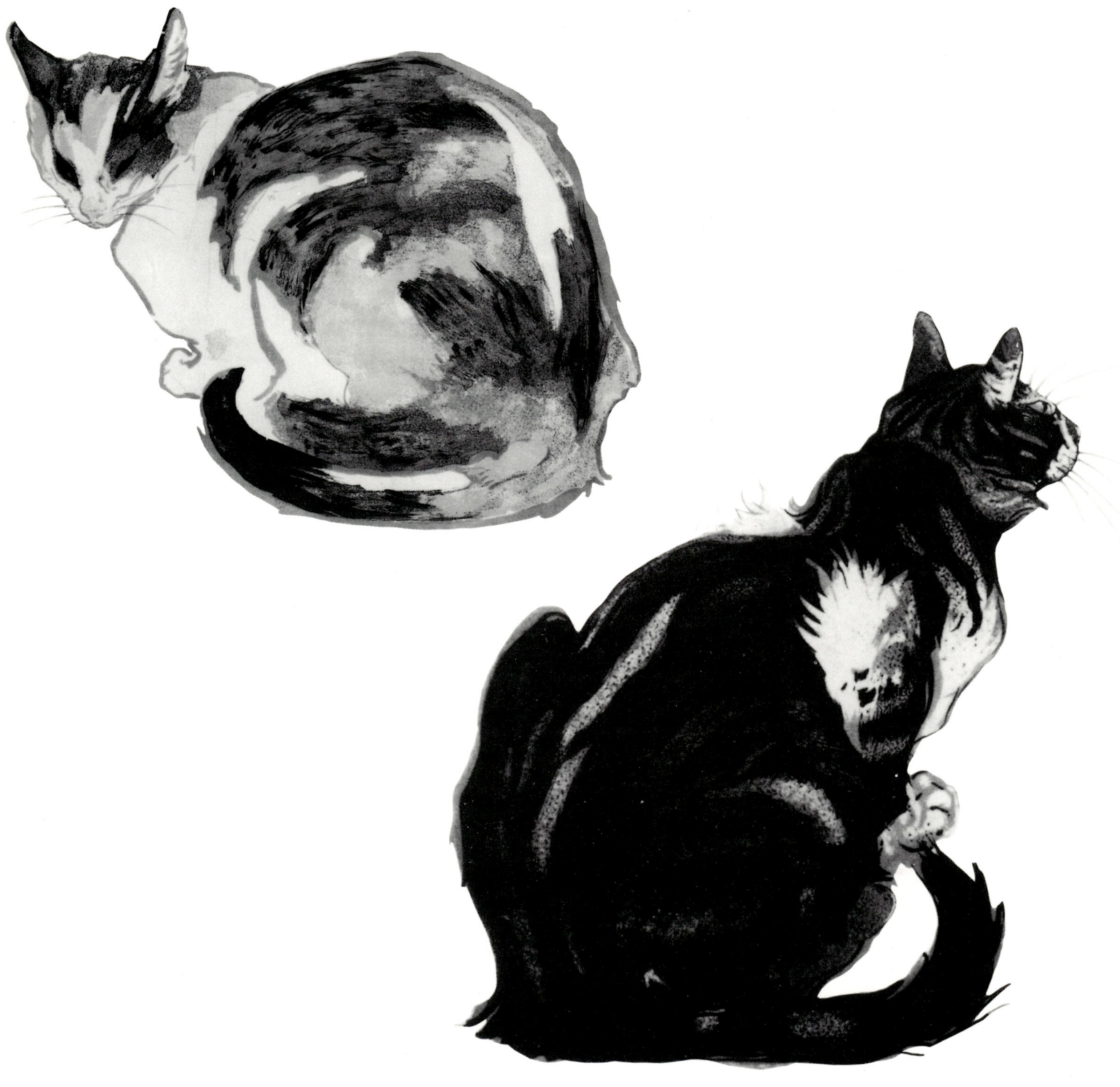

François Fossier

Curator

Print Department

Bibliothèque Nationale, Paris

Steinlen's Cats

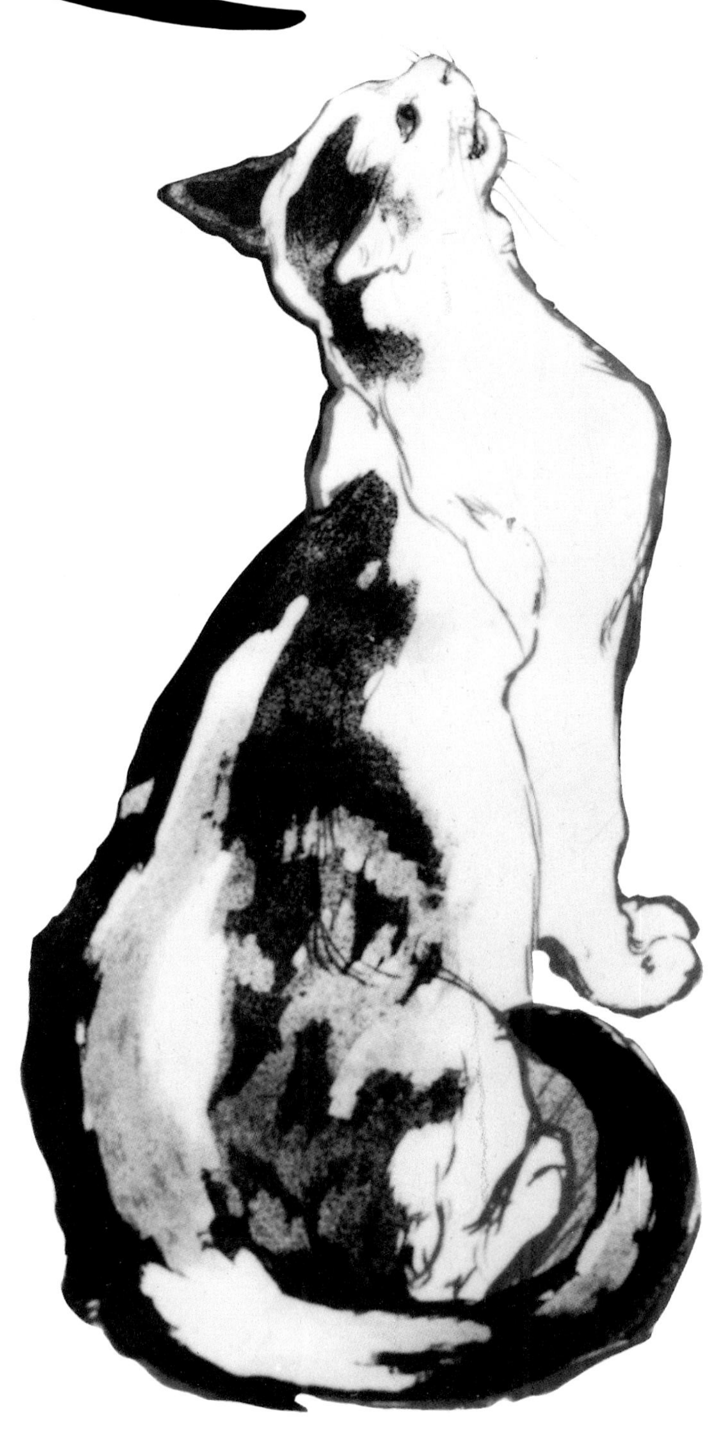

With artwork from the collections of
Bibliothèque Nationale, Paris

Harry N. Abrams, Inc., Publishers, New York

Project Director: Margaret L. Kaplan

Editor: Julia Moore

Designer: Ayn Svoboda

Library of Congress Cataloging-in-Publication Data

Fossier, François.
Steinlen's cats / François Fossier ; with artwork from the collections of Bibliothèque nationale, Paris.
p. cm.
ISBN 0-8109-2429-3
1. Steinlen, Théophile Alexandre, 1859–1923—Catalogs. 2. Cats in art—Catalogs. 3. Bibliothèque nationale (France)—Catalogs.
I. Bibliothèque nationale (France) II. Title.
NE2349.5.S74A4 1990
769.92—dc20 89-35748
CIP

Published in 1990 by Harry N. Abrams, Incorporated, New York

A Times Mirror Company

Printed and bound in Japan

CONTENTS

INTRODUCTION

Cats. Few animals unleash such violent passions, nourish so many controversies, arouse such adoration. Sacred creatures in ancient Egypt, fabled companions of ministers and bohemians, revered muses to writers, wild and scrawny protégés of old ladies in Rome, *felis domestica* has always enjoyed privilege and respect in human company.

Think of all the wills that have been drawn up in favor of cats, the fortunes bequeathed to these quite self-sufficient companions. This passion for cats has been felt—each in his own way—by Petrarch, Cardinal Richelieu, Eugène Delacroix, Charles Baudelaire, Edgar Allan Poe, Ezra Pound, Colette, and T. S. Eliot, not to mention the prophet Mohammed's glowing affection for his cat Muezza. The redoutable Samuel Johnson was a cat lover, as his faithful biographer, James Boswell, recounts: "I shall never forget the indulgence with which he treated Hodge, his cat; for whom he himself used to go out and buy oysters, lest the servants having that trouble should take a dislike to the poor creature. . . . I recollect his one day scrambling up Dr. Johnson's breast, apparently with much satisfaction, while my friend, smiling and half-whistling, rubbed down his back, and pulled him by the tail."

Cats have also had passionate detractors, including the eighteenth-century French naturalist Georges Louis Leclerc de Buffon. "The cat is a faithless domestic animal that one only keeps by necessity, as opposed to one less domestic and still more troublesome. . . . Fickle, flatterers as well as cheats, they have the same cunning, the same subtlety in doing evil, the same penchant for petty thievery. Like cheats they know how to cover their tracks, conceal their designs, spy out opportunities, wait, choose, seize the opportunity to strike, avoid punishment, flee, and keep their distance until summoned back." Clearly, Buffon resented cats' mysterious and independent ways.

An English proverb says, "The dog for the man, the cat for the woman." Through epochs of favor and disfavor, the cat has been a female symbol, and its fortunes have risen and fallen with the status of women. In the Late Middle Ages, cats were identified as agents of the devil and were put to death, sometimes with witches, by conspicuously gruesome means. Their fortunes rose, though slowly, in the Renaissance, when they began to be associated with love and devotion, and they peaked at the end of the nineteenth century, when they became highly fashionable pets in households where "ladies" were valued as domesticated objects of adornment.

"The smallest feline is a masterpiece," remarked Leonardo da Vinci, whose sheet of cat studies in the Royal Library at Windsor is often reproduced. As connoisseurs of cats, artists are in a class by themselves. Even when they do not like them, artists are sensitive to the charm of cats' playful capers, the fluid grace of their movements, and the thrilling elegance of line that defines the feline silhouette. We might even say that down through the centuries the cat in art is one of the most persistent and unchanging images and themes. Think of the many little balls of fur snoozing by the fire; the tall silhouettes, haughty and distinguished; the furies with all their claws out; the scroungers or goblins—throughout centuries of being drawn and painted, they all look like close kin.

Some of the greatest images of cats are sculptures by ancient Egyptians, for whom the cat-goddess Bastet was the major deity of motherhood and fertility as far back as 3000 B.C. In stone and wood, these large-eared, long-nosed cats sit tall, with their tails curled around them to the right. Cats crouch, doze, and leap through centuries of Chinese, Korean, and Japanese art. Symbolic cats peer out of Renaissance religious paintings by Dosso Dossi and Giulio Romano, and Domenico Ghirlandaio included a witnessing cat in his *Last Supper*. The cat becomes a natural inhabitant of seventeenth- and eighteenth-century scenes of domestic life by Dutch, French, and English painters. By the end of the nineteenth century—*la belle époque* of cat history—cats were not only worthy of independent works of art, but found their way into all kinds of paintings, posters, illustrations, and decorative objects. And it was in the Belle Epoque that cats found their most sensitive and loyal artistic champion, Théophile-Alexandre Steinlen.

Steinlen's cats are among the most perfectly understood and masterfully rendered in all of art. Steinlen captured, above all, the idea of the cat. Stretched out or curled up, leaping or creeping, gazing or sleeping, his cats are perfect expressions of catness. What did cats mean to Steinlen? And why did he put so many of them in his posters and illustrations, his etchings and lithographs? Do they all share the Mephistophelian look of the one that assured Steinlen fame during his lifetime and after: the huge, imperious black cat adorning a poster for a Montmartre cabaret? The *Tournée du Chat Noir* poster (Plate 4) is one of the most arresting images of the Belle Epoque and has long been regarded as Steinlen's most striking creation. But although the Chat Noir cat is a kind of signature piece, its black cat is absolutely not Steinlen's quintessential cat.

Some of Steinlen's other cats, to be sure, are right out of hell, but with their bullying airs and feigned indifference they strike us as comical. Others, more discreet and much more numerous, slink sinuously through Steinlen's pages. Many are celebrated as self-contained portraits of one, two, or three cats. Some are silent witnesses to scenes of human cruelty, their poignancy heightened by the cats' mute presence.

Cats appear in many scenes without playing an actual role. As subjects and objects, they circulate throughout Steinlen's work with an ambiguous ease. Sometimes they act as aesthetic counterpoints, to underscore an attitude or create contrast. But one feels that nothing escapes them, that their role goes far beyond that of balancing or harmonizing a composition in an aesthetic sense. They seem to represent Steinlen's own gaze, his judgment on what he is illustrating. He did, after all, often use the outline of a cat as part of his artistic emblems.

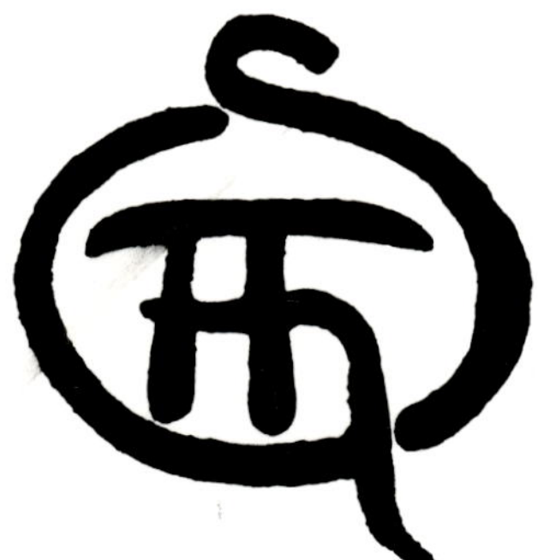

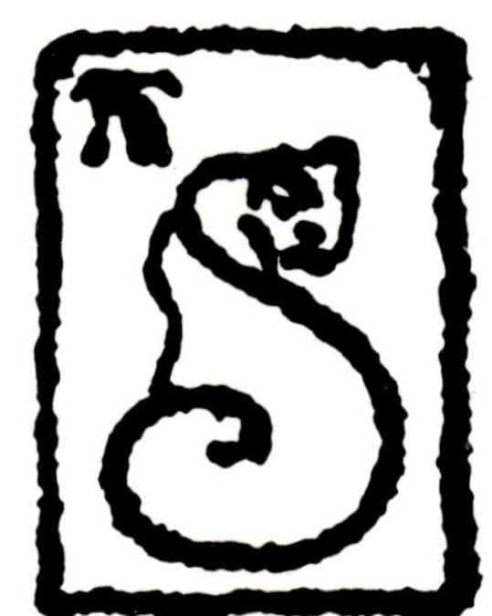

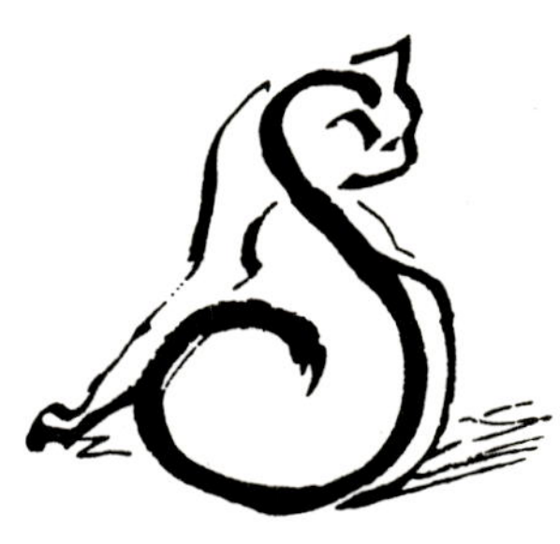

Today the name and the art of Théophile-Alexandre Steinlen are much less known than those of fellow members of the Montmartre avant-garde, such as Henri de Toulouse-Lautrec, Pierre Bonnard, and Edouard Vuillard. Yet during his most productive years, from about 1883 to the end of World War I, Steinlen was a very well known and visible artist who was admired and imitated by a younger generation of twentieth-century artists: Käthe Kollwitz, Georges Braque, and Pablo Picasso. He had a great popular following, as well, through his enormous and ceaseless output of book and magazine illustrations, posters and individual prints, sheet music covers, and decorated programs, menus, and graphic ephemera.

Steinlen was a person of many dimensions and passions, a complicated man who was drawn to the center of European intellectual and artistic life at a particularly ripe moment. He was practical and disciplined, turning out an enormous amount of work on tight deadlines. He was a committed socialist who, like Honoré Daumier before him, put his art to the idealistic service of improving the lot of the poor and disenfranchised. And there were some very personal sides to him, some qualities that reveled in the absurd, the erotic, and the irrational. It is from this side that his cats seem to have sprung.

Born in Lausanne, Switzerland in 1859, he was raised in a family that included a number of artists. His grandfather Theodore Christian Gottlieb Steinlen was a drawing teacher, lithographer, and painter of watercolor landscapes; his uncle Marius Steinlen painted enamels in Paris. Probably no one in Lausanne was surprised when the young Théophile began filling his school notebooks with drawings of cats, roosters, and other animals, an enthusiasm that was to become a lifelong study. Steinlen was an attentive, uncompromising observer of animal ways and a merciless caricaturist when he found in them the same cruelties that he abhorred in his fellow humans.

When he was twenty-one, after two restless years at the University of Lausanne, his father sent him to Mulhouse in Alsace-Lorraine to apprentice with an uncle in the textile business. There he learned how to create designs on woodblocks for printing fabrics. By the time he began his career as an illustrator, in 1883, Steinlen had four years of experience in a trade in which the design themes—a mixture of spontaneity and convention—are rooted in popular art.

In 1881 Steinlen arrived in Paris with his bride from Mulhouse, Émilie. They settled immediately in Montmartre, the district that had lured generations of creative types: artists, writers, students. What the twenty-three-year-old newcomer found in Paris, and specifically in the narrow streets of Montmartre, shocked and changed him. The sights and smells of poverty and other social injustices were far more affecting than he had imagined—even from his early reading of Émile Zola's novels. Within two years, the latent socialist from Switzerland had exchanged employment at a textile factory for the life of an artist and illustrator, partly so he could champion the cause of the downtrodden and promote his anti-capitalist convictions. Steinlen never left Montmartre and died there in 1923, long after he could have afforded a more fashionable neighborhood.

Coincidentally, another Swiss expatriot settled in Montmartre the same year that Steinlen arrived. Rodolphe Salis founded his Chat Noir cabaret in 1881 at the foot of the hill of Montmartre at 84, Rue Rochechouart. It was a new kind of cabaret, a combination political, literary, and artistic cafe that instantly became a magnet for Parisians who loved wordplay, satirical performances, politics, and modern music. Introduced to this intoxicating place in 1883 by the artist Adolphe Willette, Steinlen developed close friendships with the singer and poet Aristide Bruant, Chat Noir's headliner and the subject of several renowned posters by Toulouse-Lautrec, with the publisher Ernest Flammarion, and with Zola, to name just a few. Willette became Steinlen's inseparable comrade.

Salis's Chat Noir cabarets—the second of which opened in 1885 at 12, Rue Laval (today Rue Victor-Massé)—were the quintessence of Belle Epoque bohemianism. Salis had the genius to surround himself with talented collaborators, including Steinlen, Bruant, Willette, Émile Goudeau, and Henri Rivière, all of them natural publicists. Willette created a sign, a cat perched on a crescent moon, a stained-glass window representing the Virgin with a cat, and painted a frieze of cats on the side walls. There was no card playing or dominoes, but there were Goudeau's literary absinthe Wednesdays; Rivière's fabulous shadow-play theater performances; dinners organized by the poet-and-composer "Hydropaths," who made the Chat Noir their headquarters; Eric Satie's piano playing; and, of course, Salis's outrageous revues.

All political and literary Paris flocked there, and so did the Prince of Wales, Edgar Degas, Jules Verne, Anatole France, the photographer Félix Nadar, and Louis Pasteur. All the while, Steinlen, Caran d'Ache, Willette, Henri Pille, and others were sketching nonstop. Certain "old-timers" deplored the fact that the carefree atmosphere of the original Chat Noir had been sacrificed to a more formal tone. Salis's revue became more moderate, and he eventually organized a touring version, for which Steinlen's famous *Tournée du Chat Noir* poster (Plate 4) was designed.

It was Salis who gave Steinlen his first opportunity to publish. Part of Salis's showmanship was a weekly periodical, *Le Chat noir*, begun in 1882. Steinlen became a regular contributor with an illustration for the issue of September 1, 1883. In 1885, when Salis moved to the second address, Bruant immediately took over the old space and, seizing on Salis's idea, brought out a small newspaper bearing the name of his own cabaret, *Le Mirliton.* Later *Gil Blas illustré* commissioned Steinlen to do a large color drawing each month for its literary supplement, illustrating some story or song. Over its ten-year life, he eventually produced more than four hundred drawings for *Gil Blas illustré.* But it was tiring work with weekly deadlines, and the subjects were not always stimulating or high-minded.

Steinlen earned many opportunities to freely express his anti-capitalist views when a socialist friend, an upholsterer, founded *Le Chambard socialiste* (The Socialist Fight). The newspaper set out "to denounce without mercy social iniquities and corruptions and dirty tricks of the government." The greatest attraction of the weekly for Steinlen was its front page. Each Saturday it showed a large drawing in bold colors, signed P. P. for "Petit Pierre" (little stone), a translation of his Germanic name.

In 1897, Charles Galland, who wrote under the pen name of Zo d'Axa, offered him another forum at the anarchist periodical *La Feuille* (The Leaf). There Steinlen redressed social wrongs with seventeen strong, full-page satires in the two years of *La Feuille*'s publishing life. At these papers, and later at the socialist paper *L'Assiette au beurre* (The Butter Plate), he took as his own the statement by Charles-Louis Philippe: "I know with my eyes closed that it is the poor who are right . . . and if the poor don't make a lot of noise the rich don't even perceive that the poor exist." Steinlen's affinity for the street people of Paris was extravagantly recognized by André Warnod: "It is Steinlen's red muse who waves the red flag and breaks the chains . . . . The street is in mourning, misery, the homeless, the rain, the cold, and Steinlen's pencil is moved; the artist weeps and suffers in the street, his domain, his kingdom, his homeland."

World War I tragically offered Steinlen the opportunity to give final proof of his compassion for the poor and disinherited. For four years he turned out devastating pages in the form of posters or magazine illustrations: *The Train from Verdun*, *The Exodus*, *"Le Locataire"* (Plate 17), for example. He wielded his lithographic crayon without respite until his death in 1923.

In all he did, one can sense Steinlen's respect for his own work, and for the dignity of work as such. He provided illustrations for scores of different magazines during his career. As his reputation grew, he was increasingly sought out to produce limited-edition lithographs, and many publishers commissioned him to illustrate books. When praised for his tireless labors, he is said to have responded: "What about carpenters and bricklayers, don't they work without letup too?" Steinlen was an almost secretively hard worker. Convinced that what he saw in the streets of Paris provided the content for his work, he spent many hours each day walking, even though it meant working late at night. Daydreaming in his little garden on Montmartre's Rue Caulaincourt and playing with his daughter Colette were indispensable to his inspiration. So was playing with his cats. But at four o'clock in the morning he could be found heading to his studio to begin a full day of work.

Compared to such contemporaries as Pal (Jean Paléologue) and Tamagno, both of whom created more than three hundred posters each, Steinlen was not at all prolific as a poster artist. Toulouse-Lautrec produced at least three posters a year and Chéret twenty-five, while Steinlen averaged fewer than two a year from 1885 to his death in 1923. Steinlen's poster production is extremely diversified, however, and every one is strong. There are few stylistic points in common among the sensitive and sober *Lait de la Vingeanne* (Plate 1), the stylized *Tournée du Chat Noir* (Plate 4), and the expressive *"Le Locataire"* (Plate 17). While Jules Chéret's style developed in a regular and continuous progression, Toulouse-Lautrec's proceeded by monolithic blocks, and Alphonse Mucha's hieratic style was immutable, Steinlen's posters are highly diverse in spirit and varied in technique. And his poster designs extend over a much longer span of time than that of his colleagues: from 1885 to 1922.

The advertising assignments of his early career, such as the *Boulangerie-Pâtisserie* placard with the cat escaping from the lower-left corner (Fig. 1), were followed by the original artistic poster creations, then by bookstore posters, and finally by a somber corpus relating to World War I. The artist's first advertising illustrations hardly suggest the emotional strength of his later work. In general, they are small chromos engraved by professional lithographers who sought to render the effect of oil painting or watercolor with small dots, spots, and numerous applications of color, sometimes as many as twelve.

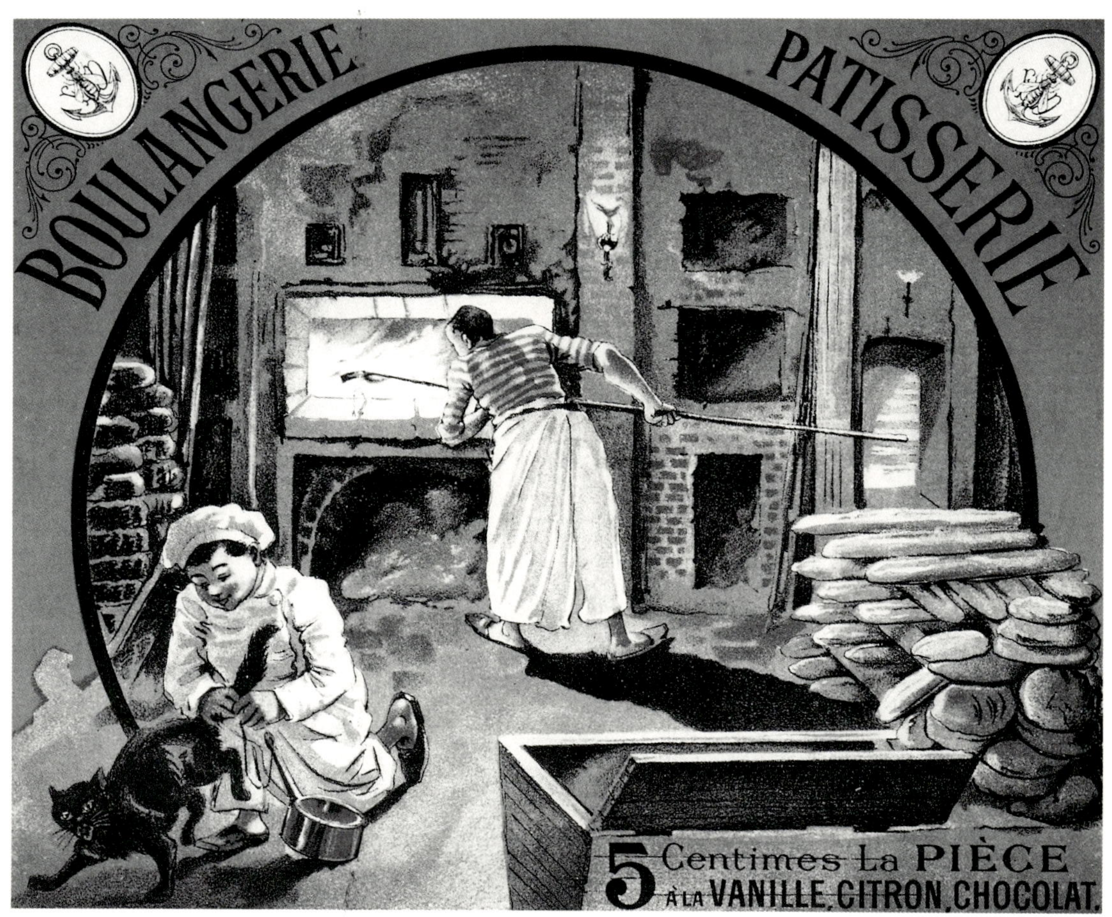

Fig. 1 *Boulangerie-Pâtisserie.* 1889. Lithographic placard, 7⅞ x 9 in. (20 x 23 cm). Printer: Mazrand et Cie., Paris. Crauzat 487; Bargiel/Zagrodzki 8

Beginning in 1890, Steinlen's style was influenced by Japanese prints, which had been promoted by dealer Siegfried Bing's periodical *Le Japon artistique.* That same influence had been apparent for some fifteen years in Manet's prints, Chéret's posters, and Henri Rivière's wood engravings. Charles Gillot, a great lover and collector of Japanese art, introduced Steinlen not only to his new photomechanical process, *gillotage*, which Steinlen was to make use of in his 1898 album *Des Chats* (Some Cats), but also to the art of interrupted perspectives, plunging views, flat colors, and such themes of Japanese inspiration as cats. His first poster in the Japonisme genre, *Le Rêve* (The Dream) of 1890 (Fig. 2), is a bit confused and crowded. But Steinlen's style progressed quickly toward refinement, and with his 1893 *Mothu et Doria* (Fig. 3) it rose in a single stroke to top rank. (The debt to Toulouse-Lautrec's 1892 *Ambassadeurs: Aristide Bruant* is obvious, but the style is a personal one.) Economy of means, bold cropping, brush and spatter technique—which he used consistently after 1892—and an aesthetic that was simultaneously simple and refined: these are hallmarks of a master of the art poster who emerged in the years 1893–96.

Steinlen's black-and-white drawings, appearing at the same time in *Gil Blas illustré*, are in no way inferior to his larger works in color. Steinlen, like Jean-Louis Forain and Adolphe Willette, proved to be a brilliant caricaturist. His use of line was sure and unerring, and he was able to synthesize graphic elements to convey visual meaning instantly

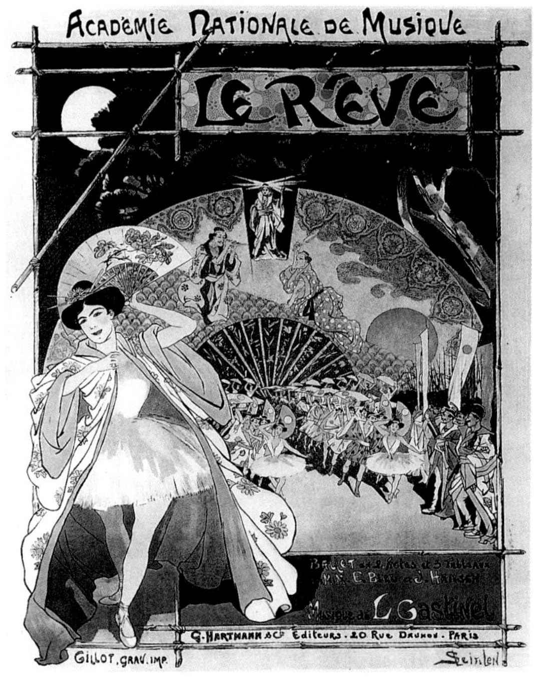

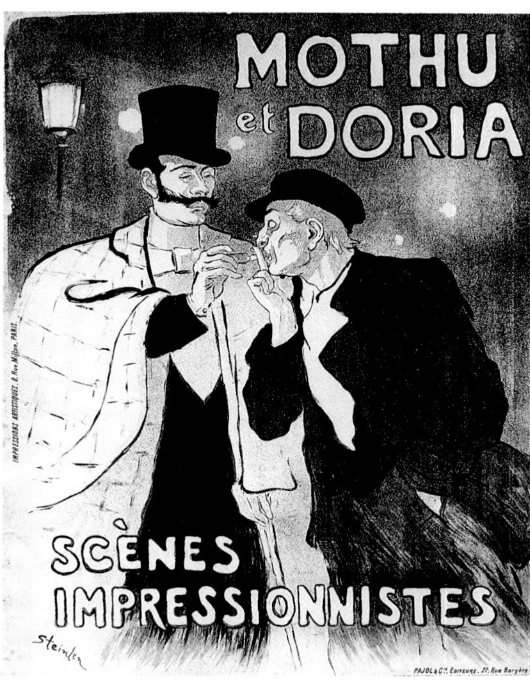

Fig. 2 *Le Rêve* (The Dream). 1890. *Gillotage*-printed poster, 33 x 24¾ in. (84 x 63 cm). Printer: Gillot, Paris. Crauzat 530; Bargiel/Zagrodzki 10

Fig. 3 *Mothu et Doria.* 1893. Lithographic poster, 51¼ x 37 in. (130 x 94 cm). Printer: Impressions Artistiques, Paris. Crauzat 490; Bargiel/Zagrodzki 12

and powerfully. Street scenes, scenes of children, and portraits of animals multiplied in his work. He rendered each theme with a suitable technique, for inspiration and the means of expressing it came naturally to him. Abandoning the photomechanical *gillotage* used for *Le Rêve,* he began attacking the stone directly by practicing "raw" lithography, replacing the pen of the transfer litho with the thick and greasy lithographic crayon. This prohibited all second thoughts and imparted great softness to his images. The nervous shading of his early newspaper drawings gave way to more suppleness and density, leading to such perfect results as *Chanson frêle* (Frail Song, Fig. 4), from the 1897 book *Chansons de Femmes* (Songs of Women).

The cat in *Chanson frêle* is typically Steinlenesque in the role it plays. The image of indifference and of fate, the lounging cat both echoes and mocks the sadness of the frail young woman. Wherever Steinlen put them, his cats embody better than anything else can the alternation between indifference and tenderness, innocent play and fierce struggle, nonchalance and erotic sensuality. Steinlen knew how to depict them by themselves, given over to their games, their indolence, or in counterpoint to an intrigue in which they are not directly involved. While the streets offered a spectacle of cruelty, extravagance, and affection that his cats could mirror, his interiors often portray an image of life in which—catlike—misery, violence, and peaceful happiness coexist. The seemingly innocent vignettes of people with cats or children are full of deeper and sometimes tragic meaning.

A number of contemporaries and rivals took up Steinlen's cat theme. Among them were his colleague at *L'Assiette au beurre,* Paul Balluriau, whose work is almost a pastiche of Steinlen's; his only pupil, Clémentine Hélène Dufau; his compatriot Edouard Morenod, alias Regina Badet; and many young American commercial artists receptive to European

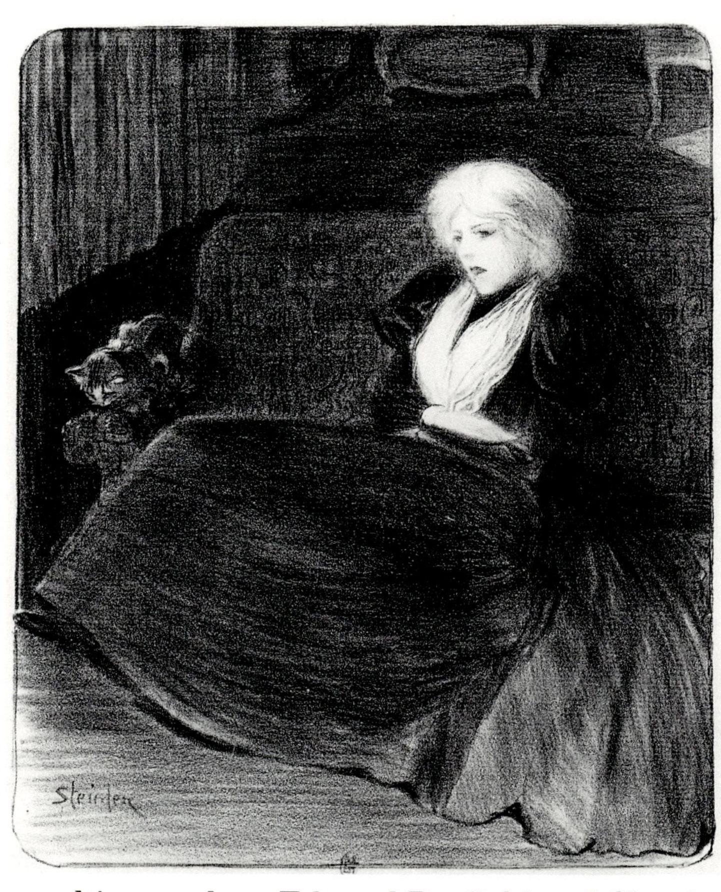

Fig. 4 *Chanson frêle,* from *Chansons de Femmes.* 1897. Lithographic illustration, 7⅞ x 6⅜ in. (20 x 16 cm). Printer: Eug. Verneau, Paris. Crauzat 194

novelties, such as Edward Penfield and Claude Fayette Bragdon. In Spain, Ramón Casas, a poster artist of a realist persuasion who had worked for *Le Chat noir* and *Gil Blas illustré,* shows the same simple composition, the same supple and powerful line, the same type of women. Isidro Nonell in Barcelona provided drawings for *Els Quatre Gats* (The Four Cats), a newspaper imitating *Gil Blas illustré,* that look like copies of Steinlen's, while Torres Garcia in *El Gato Negro* (Black Cat) imitated Steinlen's imperious *Tournée du Chat Noir* cat.

Steinlen's relative obscurity today contrasts with the fame he enjoyed during his lifetime. While he lived, his drawings were where he wanted them to be, quite literally in the hands of the masses—in magazines, books, book covers, sheet music, programs, menus, and invitations. His charming and mischievous "stories without words," including *Des Chats,* were immensely popular (Fig. 5). He was a leading printmaker and poster designer and was represented by dealer Edouard Kleinmann, who also handled the posters of Toulouse-Lautrec, Willette, Chéret, Forain, and others of the artistic vanguard. In 1894, he had a large one-man show of paintings and drawings at Galerie La Bodinière (see back cover), and he exhibited at least once more with other animal specialists (see Fig. 11). Ten years before his death, his importance was recognized by the Society for the Propagation of Art Books, which published a 232-page illustrated *catalogue raisonné* by one of its members, writer and print collector Ernest de Crauzat.

That Steinlen concentrated his energy on the anti-elitist graphic arts instead of on painting probably accounts for history's benign neglect of him. He was a powerful and very prolific draftsman, an eye endowed with a soul. In technical skill and expressive power, he was the equal of any of his contemporaries. But just as paintings are valued more than drawings and illustrations, so are painters held in greater esteem than graphic artists. In the end, it is his cats that have secured him a special place of endearment, perhaps because he rarely included them in his discomforting illustrations for political and social causes. His greatest cat images date before 1905; his most powerful social statements date after 1905. Social passions are often specific to their times. Cats are forever. Immutable, they doze, arch their backs, squint knowingly. We can almost hear them purr and hiss.

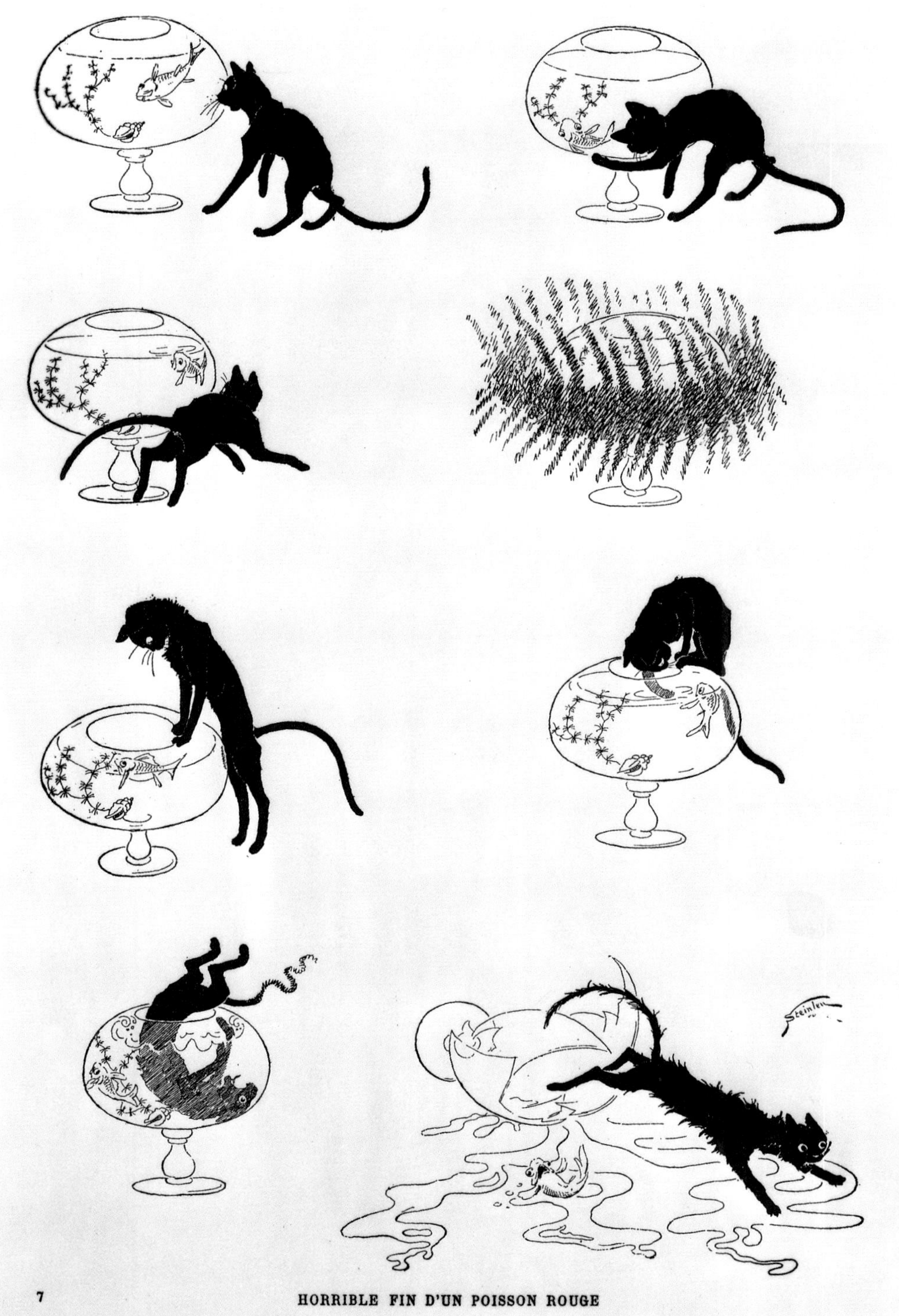

Fig. 5 *Horrible fin d'un poisson rouge*, Pl. 7 from *Des Chats.* 1898. Ernest Flammarion, Paris. Crauzat 598

THE PLATES

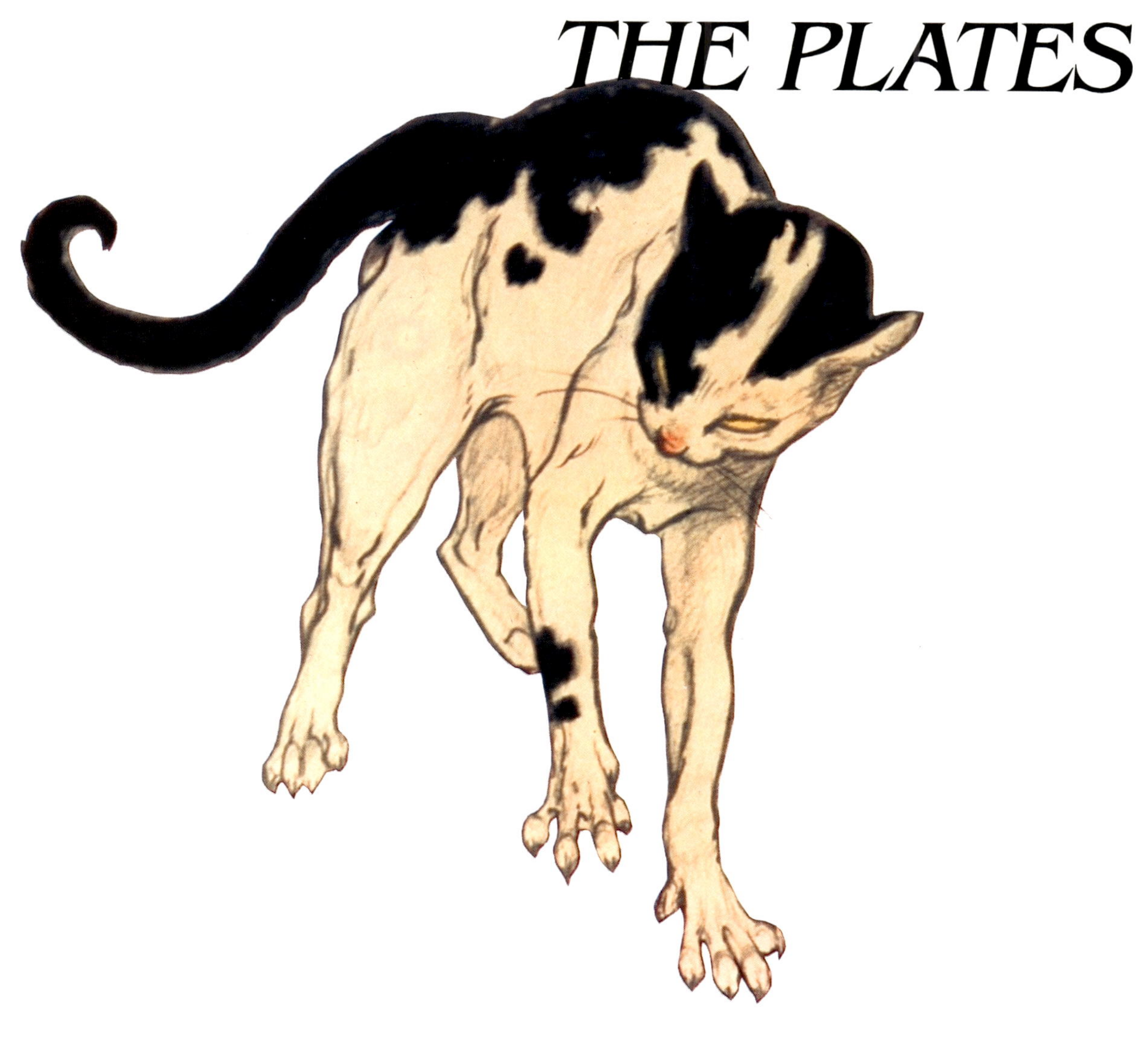

Plate 1

LAIT PUR STÉRILISÉ DE LA VINGEANNE Pure Sterilized Milk from the Vingeanne Region

1894

Using his daughter Colette and a trio of his pet cats as models, Steinlen created this classic domestic encounter to advertise milk from the Vingeanne region. A demure and cautious Colette sips from an overlarge bowl, keeping a wary eye on the three greedy creatures who make eyes at her. The tiger cat has already put a taloned paw on her fancy red dress. The emboldened black cat, back raised, is getting ready to follow suit, while the tabby impatiently beats his tail on the floor. Despite the apparent charm of the scene, there is real tension: Will the cats leap up, attack Colette, and take the milk for themselves?

In a sense, Steinlen's cats began with this poster masterpiece. He did not draw cats as primary subjects until 1894 (see back cover), by which time his career was firmly established. This is also the first piece printed for Steinlen by Charles Verneau, a leading printer with whom he established a long and rewarding business relationship. The lithograph is worked with brush, spatter technique, and scraper in orange, red, olive, green, and black, and had five large printings during its first year of issue. There are fourteen different lithographic variants of this classic image, including two that advertise Nestlé's Swiss Milk (Bargiel/Zagrodzki 17) and the oversize version before lettering on the front cover of this book.

Color lithographic poster
54¾ x 39⅜ inches (139 x 100 cm)
Printer: Charles Verneau, Paris

Crauzat 491; Bargiel/Zagrodzki 16:A1

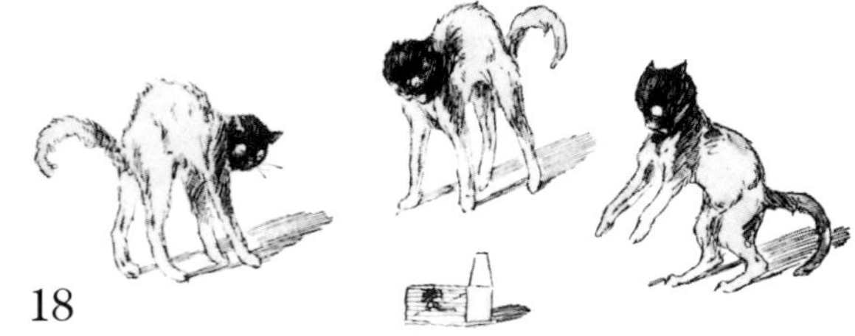

Lait pur de la Vingeanne
Stérilisé

Quillot frères
Montigny sur Vingeanne
Côte d'Or

Steinlen

Imp. CHARLES VERNEAU, 114 Rue Oberkampf. PARIS. (DEPOSE)

Plate 2

CHOCOLATS C[IE] FRANÇAISE

Française Chocolate Company

1895

Golden-haired Colette, a year older than in the Vingeanne milk poster, is determined to defend her bowl of chocolate. This time she has only one adversary, but what a one! Its throat swollen with desire, its hindquarters forming an acute angle under the tension of its muscles, it attempts one last maneuver to wheedle what it wants: it tries to stare down the little girl. Colette grasps her spoon firmly in her left hand and protects the bowl with her right arm. Unaware of the tabletop drama, the mother is lost in thought, her empty cup held loosely in her fingers.

Interestingly, Steinlen made a preparatory sketch for this scene, now in the Drawing Department of the Louvre, which has no cat (Fig. 6). In it, an affectless little Colette is hunched over her cup, while her mother seems to be admonishing her. By introducing the cat, Steinlen brilliantly exploited the tension posed by the covetous cat to make the product—hot chocolate—seem the more precious.

The lithograph, done with brush and spatter technique, was printed by the Courmont brothers in two versions, the smaller, borderless one with the lettering "Compagnie Française des Chocolats et des Thés" printed in the field above the heads (Fig. 7), and the one reproduced in color here, with its distinctive chocolate-brown border.

Color lithographic poster
47¼ x 31⅕ inches (120 x 80 cm)
Printer: M. Lasas, Paris

Crauzat 494; Bargiel/Zagrodzki 19:C

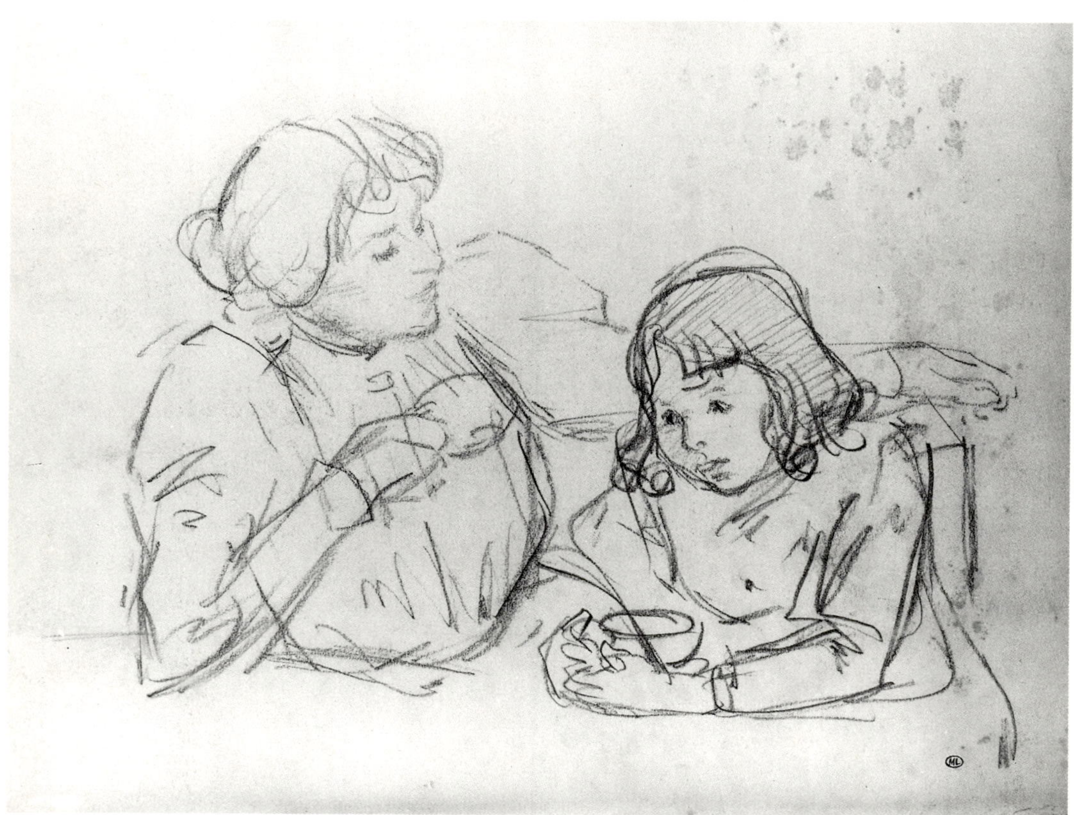

Fig. 6 *Young Girl and Mother.* c. 1895. Sketch. Drawing Department, The Louvre (RF 33830)

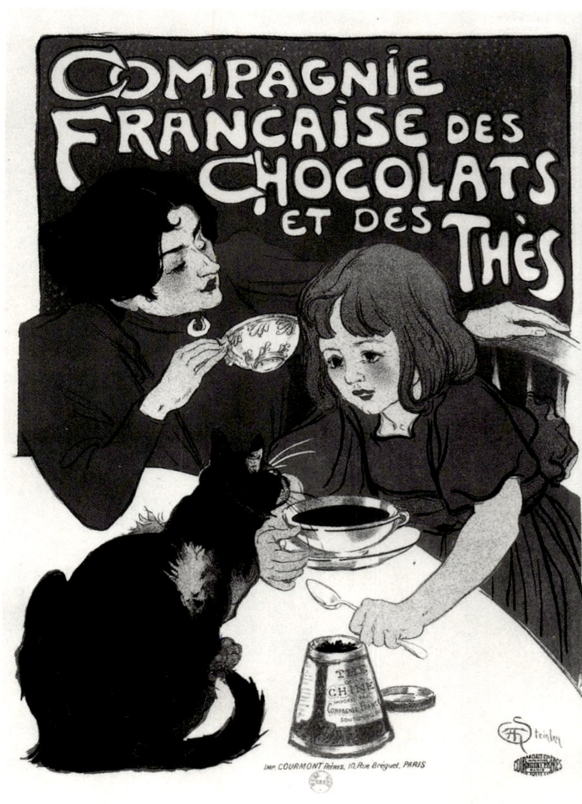

Fig. 7 *Compagnie Française des Chocolats et des Thés.* 1895. Lithographic poster, 31½ x 10⅝ in. (80 x 27 cm). Printer: Courmont Frères, Paris. Crauzat 494; Bargiel/Zagrodzki 19:A

CHOCOLATS

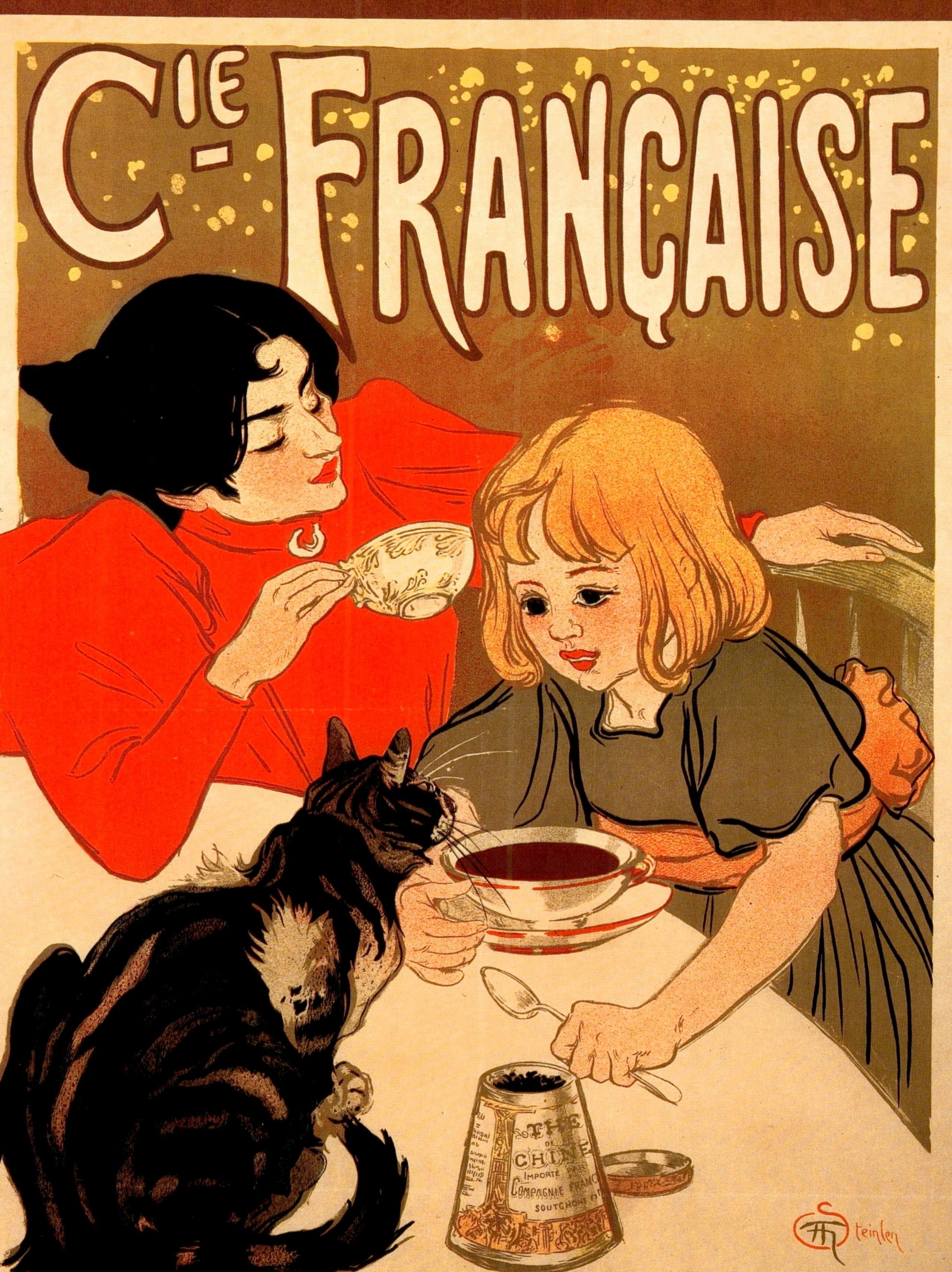

THÉS Cie FRANÇAISE

IMP. H. LAAS, 16, R. PIERRE-LEVÉE. PARIS

Plate 3

MASSON CHOCOLATIER CALENDAR PAGE

1896

Colette's third appearance is more melancholy than the first two. The little girl has been sick. She is still wan, and compliantly drinks her "Papilla mexicaine" while sitting in a pillow-stuffed wicker armchair. At her feet is a page of a book that will be published two years later, her father's *Des Chats* (see Plates 5 and 6 and Fig. 5); the stiff feet of her Japanese doll prop up the cover. But it is the tabby cat that gets Colette's attention. Tentatively raising a paw, it implores with a restraint that is appropriate to the sickroom.

Steinlen was one of twelve artists—each one furnishing an illustration for a different month—who contributed to the Masson chocolate factory's advertising calendar for the year 1896.

Lithograph with type
8⅝ x 6½ inches (22 x 16 cm)
Printer: G. de Malherbe, Paris

Crauzat 738; Bargiel/Zagrodzki 94

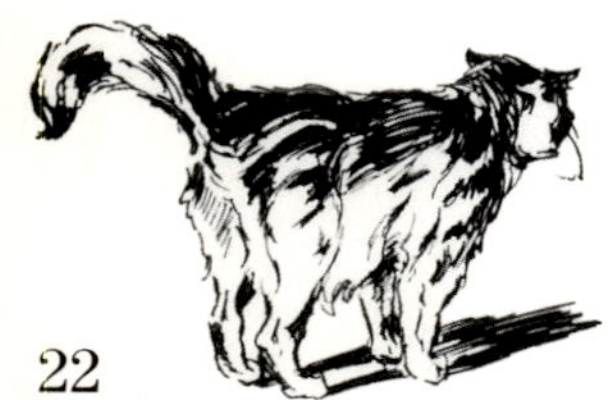

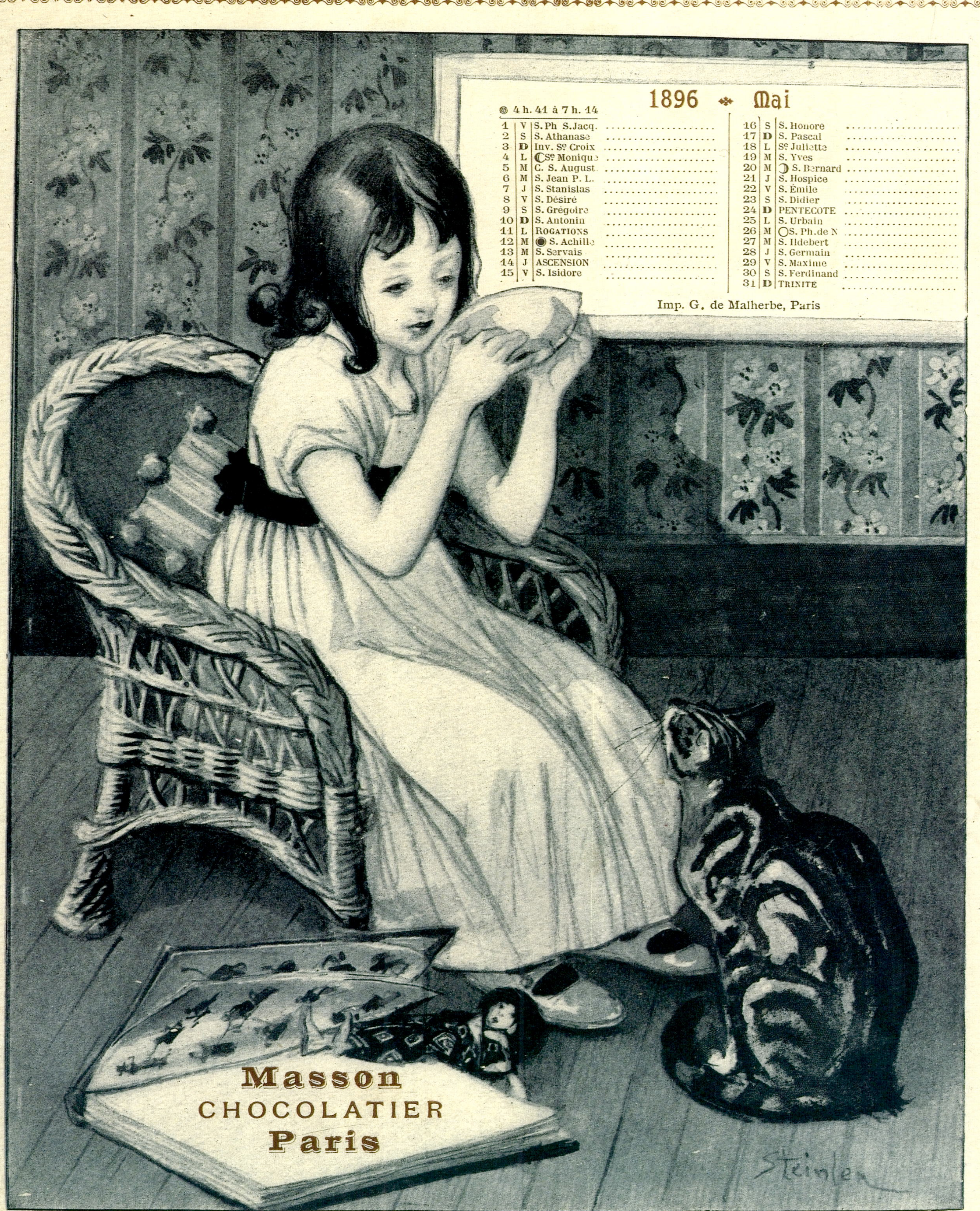

Bébé, un peu éprouvé par les premières chaleurs, ne prend plus avec plaisir que sa « PAPILLA MEXICAINE »

CHOCOLAT MEXICAIN, PEU SUCRÉ, LE PLUS DIGESTIF

Plate 4

TOURNÉE DU CHAT NOIR

Chat Noir Tour

1896

"Coming Soon: Chat Noir Tour with Rodolphe Salis." Whiskers perfectly symmetrical, pupils reduced to slits, claws out, and fur stiff, this incarnation of Beelzebub—haloed by Salis's legend "Montjoye Montmartre," a variation of the historical French war cry "Montjoie Saint Denis"—commands rather than invites. Printed in only two colors, this most arresting of Steinlen's posters is a clash of compositional restraint and expressive power. All the strength and originality of Steinlen's art is here, in the layout, the colors, the powerful and economical drawing of the cat. This *chat noir* is wild and dangerous, which is surely what Salis wanted to suggest of his touring show.

In fact, by the time Steinlen was commissioned to do this poster, the Chat Noir had been in existence for fifteen years and was well past its heyday. Beginning in 1892, Salis took a show on the road to the larger cities of the French provinces, and to Switzerland, Belgium, Algeria, and Tunisia. Smaller variations of this poster advertise "the very illustrious company of the Chat Noir with its celebrated shadow plays, its poets, its composers with Rodolphe Salis." The tours were only moderately successful, and they exhausted Salis. Ill and worn out, he closed the Montmartre cabaret in 1895, but reopened it in October of 1896. He announced a tour to Russia, but died in March 1897 before it got under way. The halo effect of the cabaret's magic spread to such unlikely enterprises as a shoe shop, for which Steinlen designed a receipt form (Fig. 8). In it, the haughty black angora takes charge of the moonlit Paris skyline like a spook in the night.

Color lithographic poster
55¾ x 39⅜ inches (142 x 100 cm)
Printer: Charles Verneau, Paris

Crauzat 496; Bargiel/Zagrodzki 22:A1

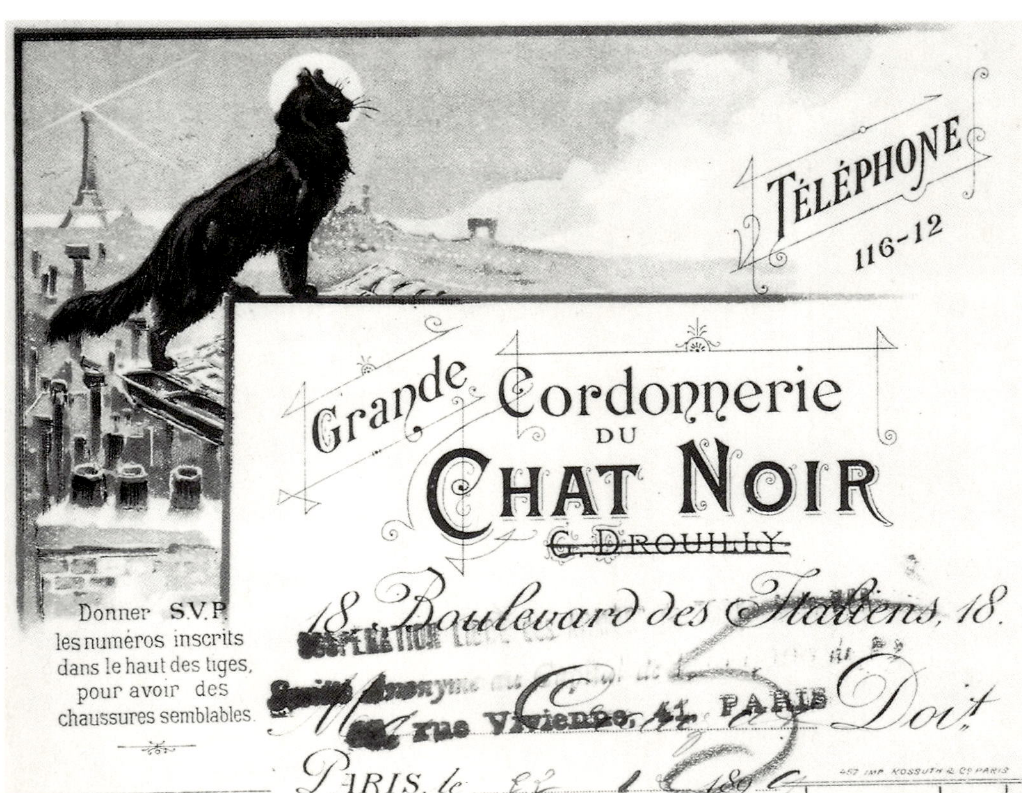

Fig. 8 *Receipt letterhead for Grande Cordonnerie du Chat Noir* (Black Cat Shoemakers). c. 1899. 8¼ x 5⅜ in. (21 x 13.5 cm). Crauzat 740; Bargiel/Zagrodzki 90

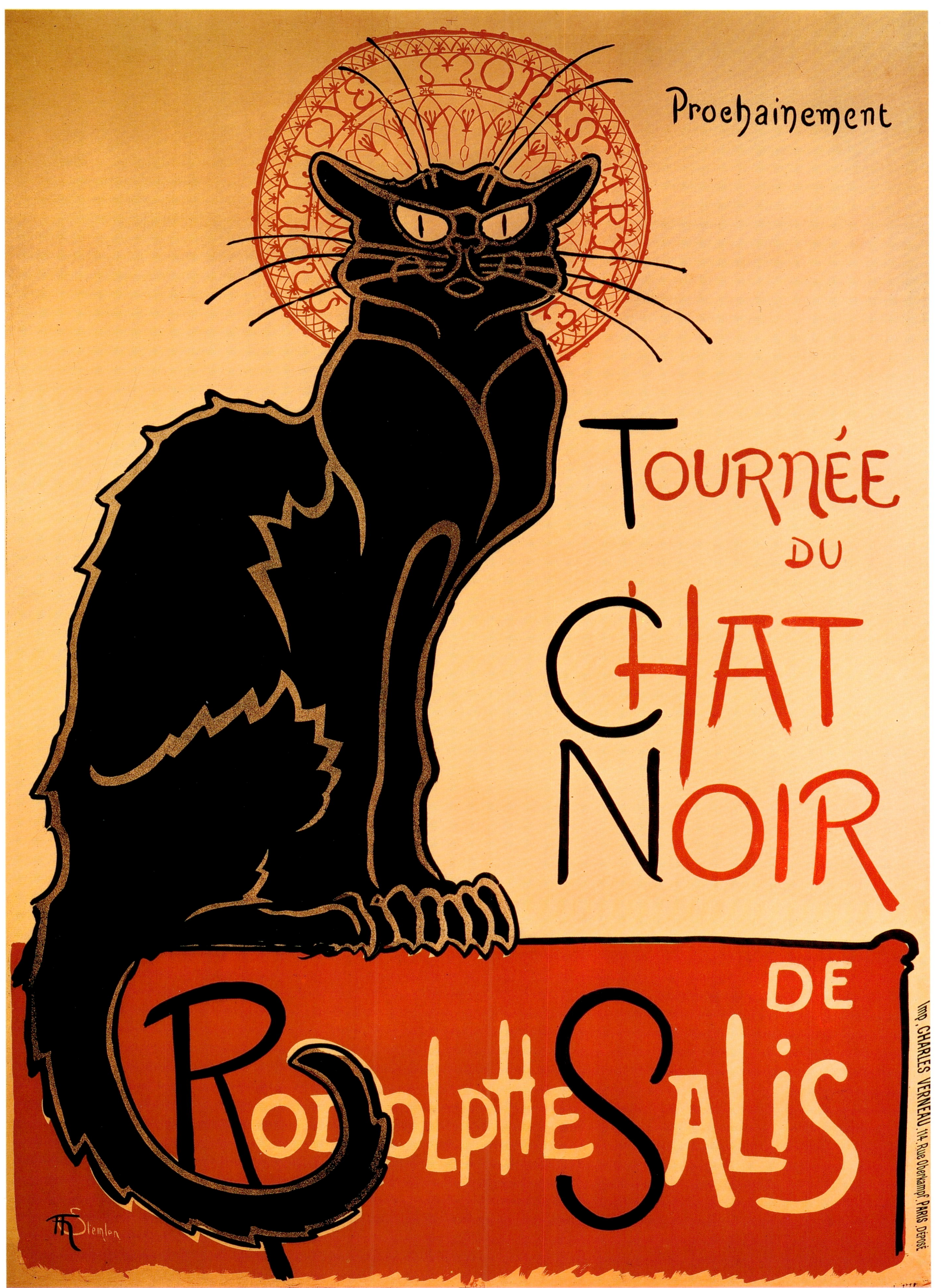
Prochainement
Tournée
du
Chat
Noir
de
Rodolphe Salis
Steinlen
Imp. CHARLES VERNEAU, 114, Rue Oberkampf, PARIS, DÉPOSÉ

Plate 5

DES CHATS FRONT COVER

Some Cats

1898

Colette reappears again, this time with a bowl of milk meant for the cats. By now the tabby and black cat are quite familiar characters. Hers is a brave act, for the six assorted demons are conspiring to wrest the dish from her. They have set up a wailing chorus. One leans into her; the tiger cat's front paws grab her almost at the waist, and three more cats block her way. This time the drama is whether she will spill the milk under the furies' assault.

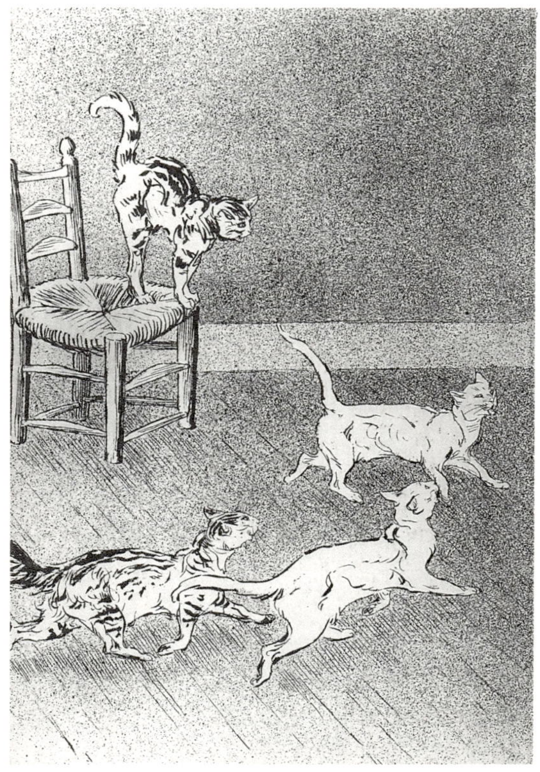

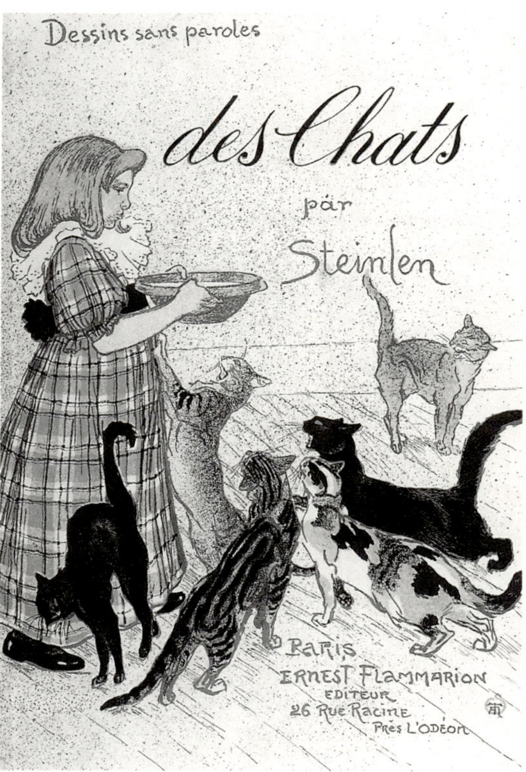

Des Chats, one of Steinlen's original "stories without words," was published in 1898. It consists of twenty-six *gillotage* plates, which had first been published in *Le Chat noir,* each page illustrating a cat drama in a sequence of black-and-white line drawings and silhouettes that brilliantly and effortlessly capture cats' grace and silliness. (A page can be previewed in miniature in the open book in the Masson Chocolatier calendar page, Plate 3, and in Fig. 5. Various cats from *Des Chats* play in the margins of this book.)

Color lithograph
18⅛ x 12⅜ inches (46 x 31 cm)
Printer: Ch. Verneau, Paris

Crauzat 215

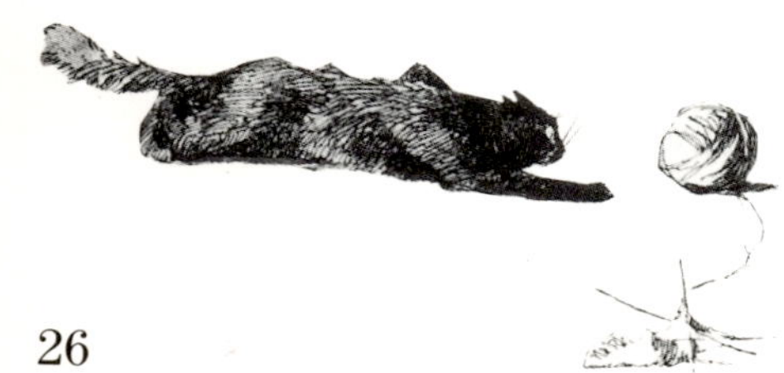

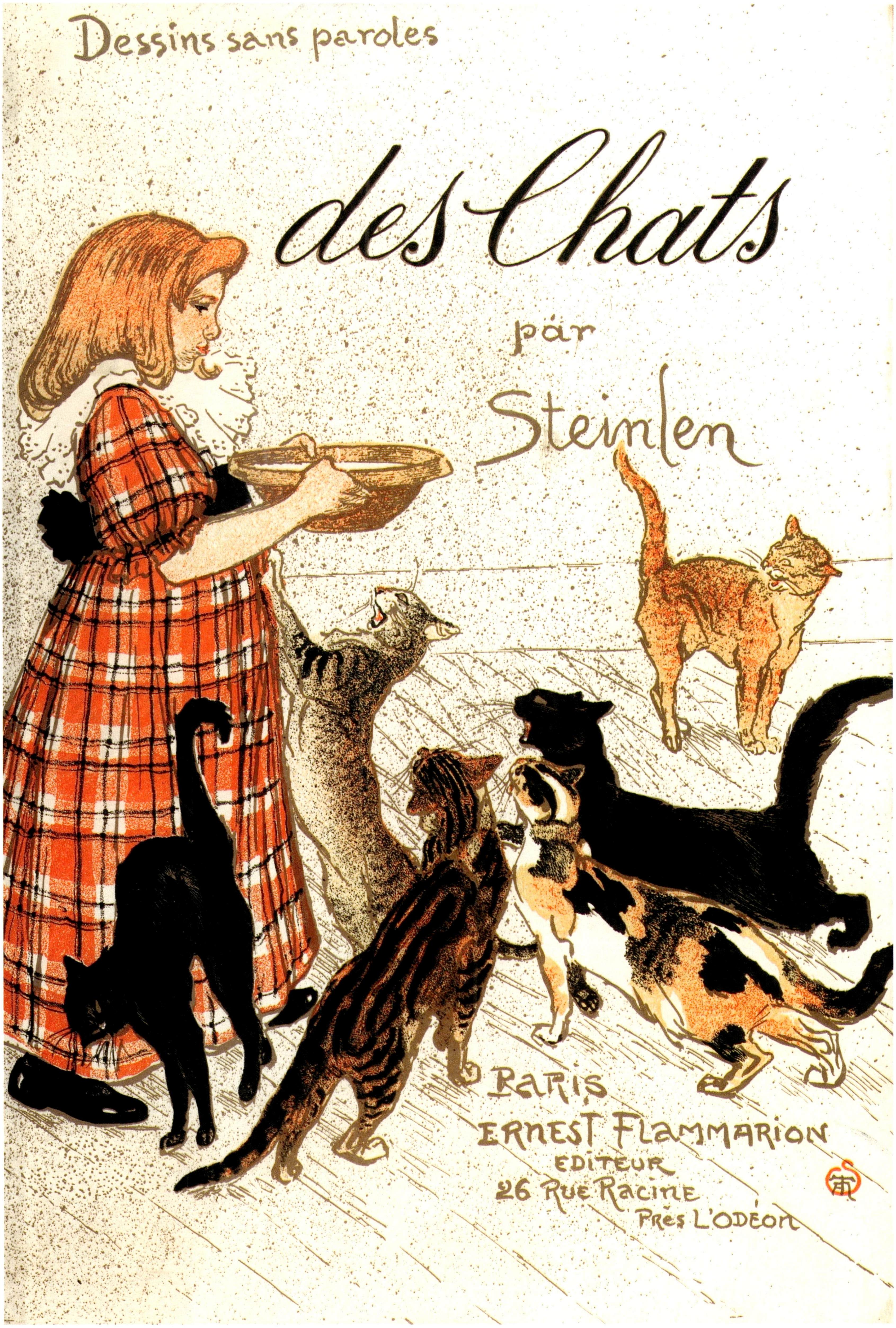

Dessins sans paroles

des Chats

par

Steinlen

PARIS
ERNEST FLAMMARION
EDITEUR
26 RUE RACINE
PRES L'ODEON

Plate 6

DES CHATS BACK COVER
Some Cats
1898

Here, in a surprise attack on the unseen Colette, are four more cats. Their strategy is perfectly clear when the book lies open and facedown. With the kindness of cheetahs, the four cats race from behind the embattled child to "lend a paw" to their six howling companions on the front cover. This plate, in fact, is often referred to as "The Cat Race."

Des Chats was published by the great French house of Ernest Flammarion, whose owner Steinlen had met years before when they both frequented Rodolphe Salis's Chat Noir cabaret.

Lithograph
18⅛ x 12⅜ inches (46 x 31 cm)
Printer: Ch. Verneau, Paris

Crauzat 216

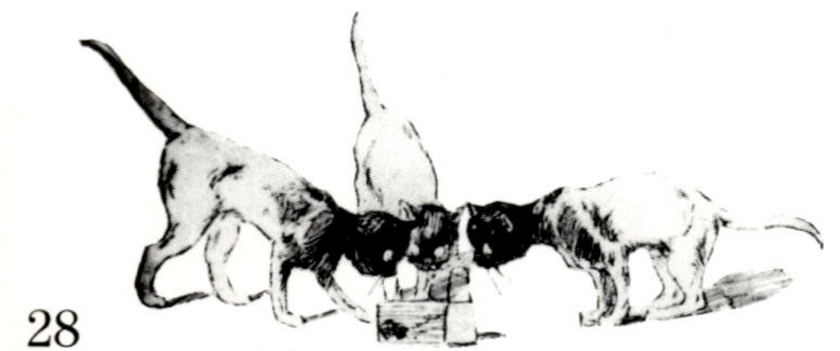

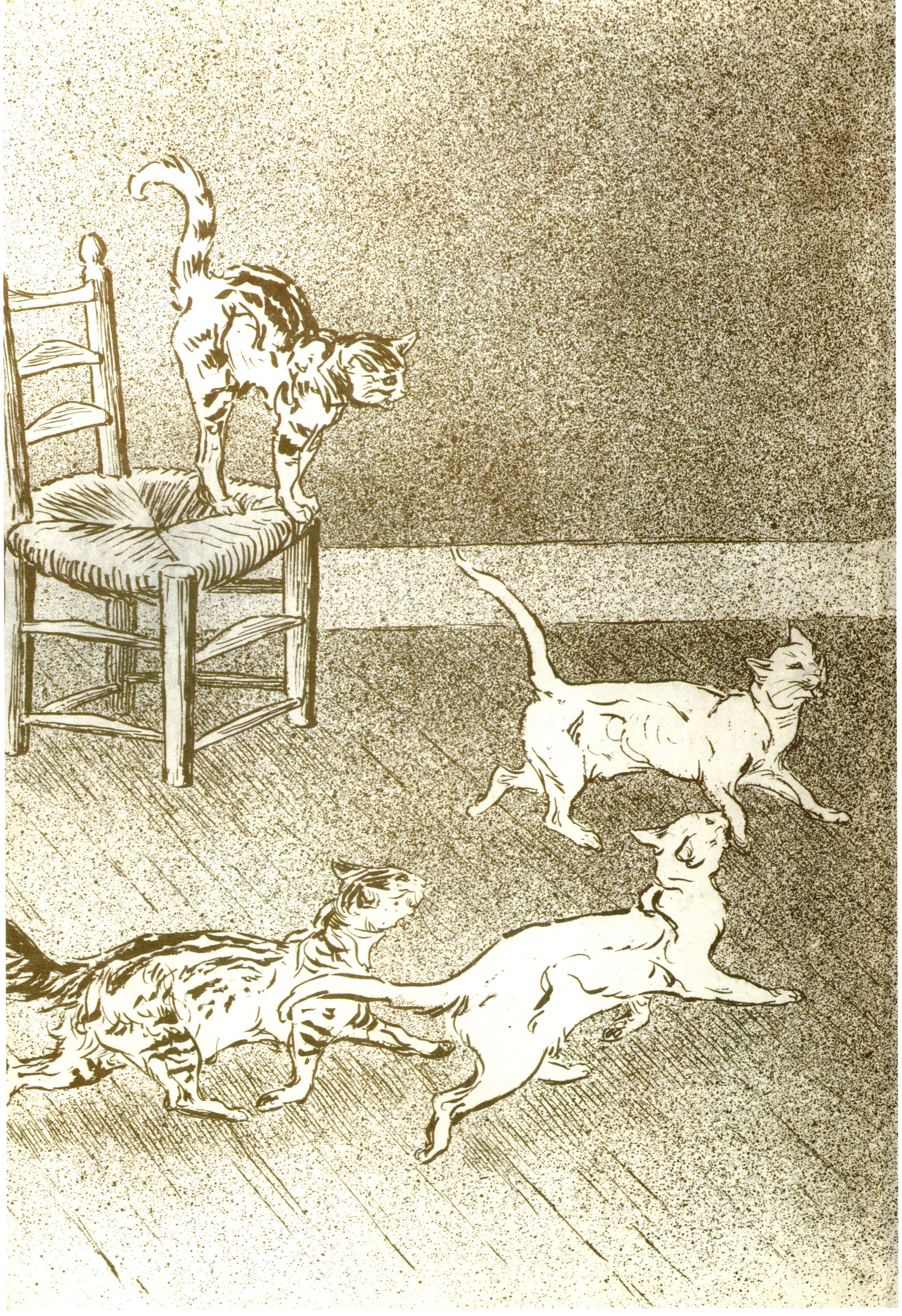

Plate 7

TWO CATS ON A CUSHION

1898

Two cats on a cushion sleep back to front, the paw of one curled with astonishing fidelity of gesture. Compared to the malevolent creatures in Steinlen's earlier posters, these two are pictures of quietude. Everything about this small print is quiet: the horizontality, the composition, even the colors. It is worthy of Whistler for its elegance and skillful, velvet-rich handling of blacks. Steinlen was a master of the etched zinc plate, and the first two states, which are black-and-white only and do not have the striped curtain backdrop, are beautiful studies in dark on light.

Etching and aquatint on zinc
6 x 9 inches (15 x 23 cm)
Third state of three

Crauzat 29

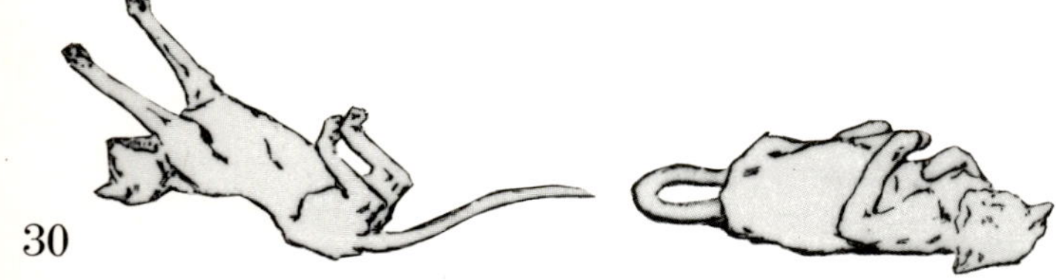

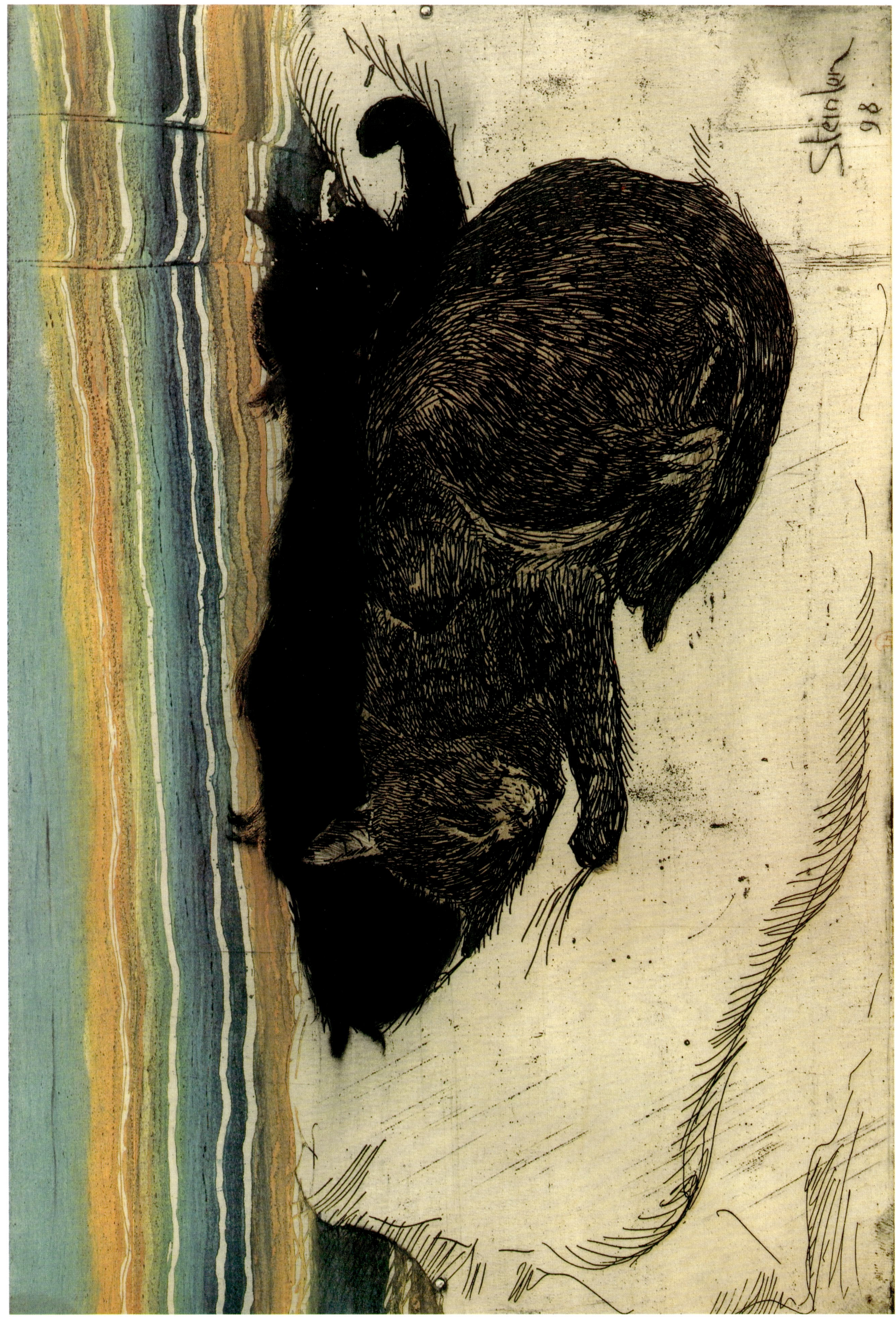

Plate 8

SMALL CAT

1898

Wet-nosed and well-fed, the diminutive tabby could be either young or small, or both. It lies on its side, facing forward and rounding its back, with its white throat, nose, and paws standing out against its soft, mottled fur. In the upper-right corner, Steinlen inscribed a dedication with his etching needle:

A l'ami Eug. Delâtre
ce premier cuivre—résultat de ses
bons conseils et de la gentillesse de
son petit chat—est dédié.
Juin 98
Steinlen

To friend Eug[ene] Delâtre
this first copper etching—resulting from his
good advice and the sweetness of
his little cat—is dedicated.

Drypoint etching with color on copper
4 x 6½inches (10 x 16 cm)
Third state of three

Crauzat 27

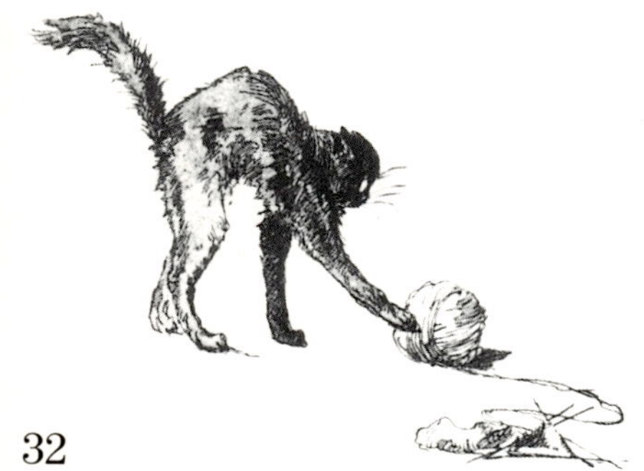

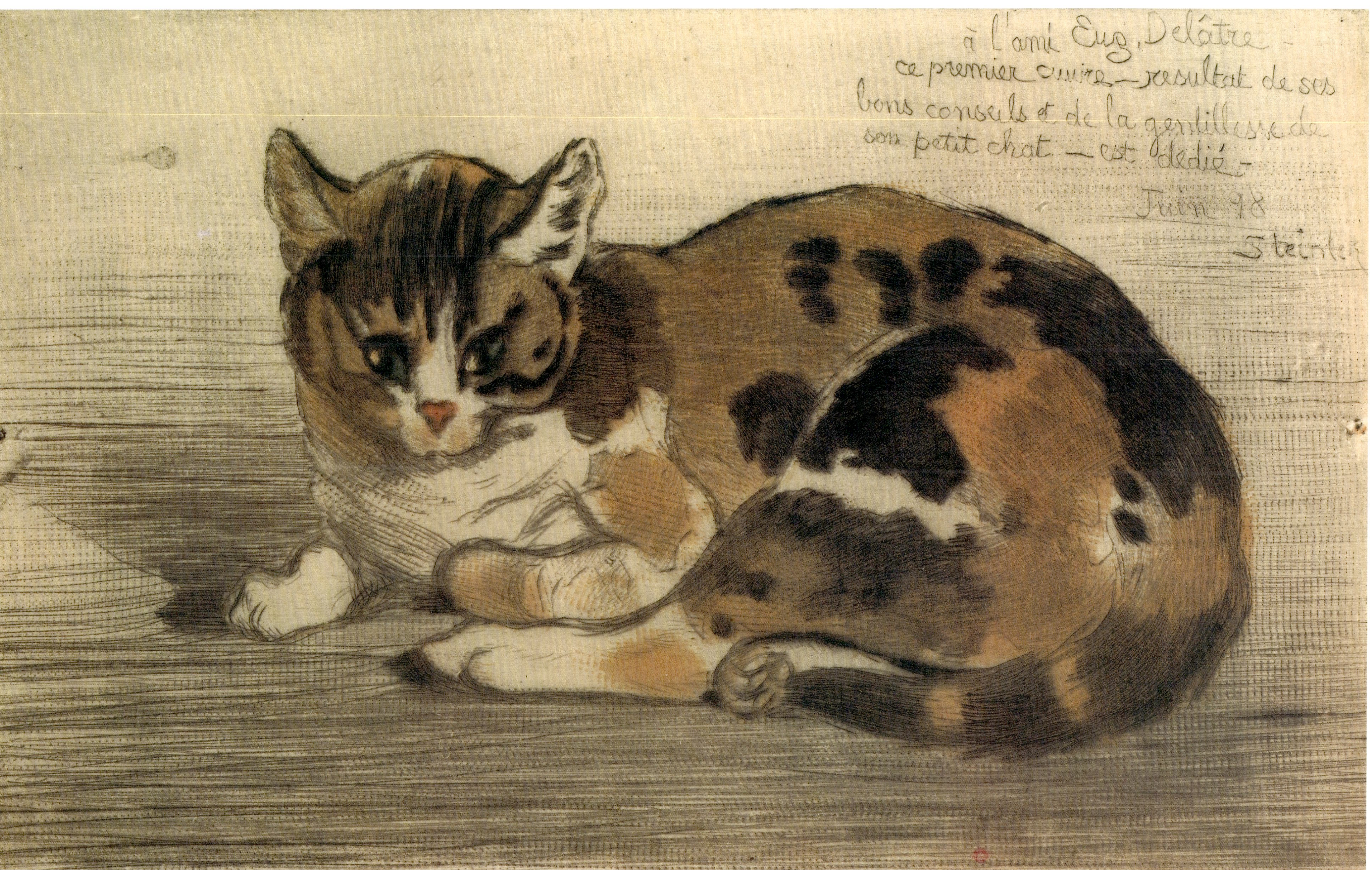
à l'ami Eug. Delâtre –
ce premier cuivre – resultat de ses
bons conseils et de la gentillesse de
son petit chat – est dédié –
Juin 98
Steinlen

Plate 9

CAT DOZING IN A CORNER

1902

Propped against the wall with its plain vertical stripes, the cat rests its head at the corner, all four paws voluptuously extended. The position may look uncomfortable, but it is one that cats sometimes adopt in defiance of logic and comfort. It is also a very Japanese composition.

The year 1902 witnessed the creation of Steinlen's finest cats. He produced a number of etchings—probably collectable art prints—in which he explored their characteristic positions and gestures with a true cat lover's affection.

Soft-ground etching, aquatint, and drypoint on zinc
7 x 7⅞ inches (18 x 20 cm)
Third state of three

Crauzat 76

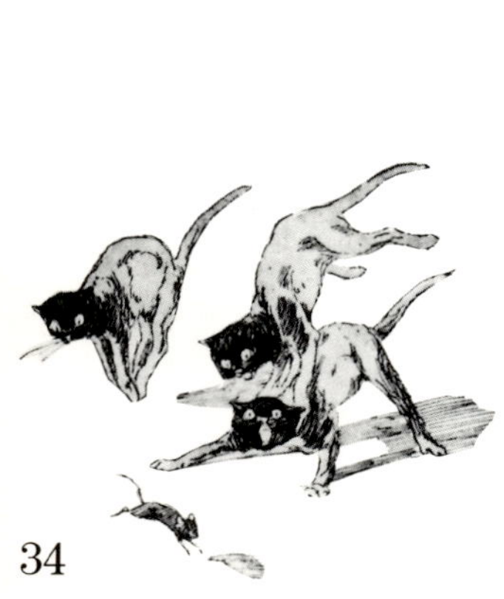

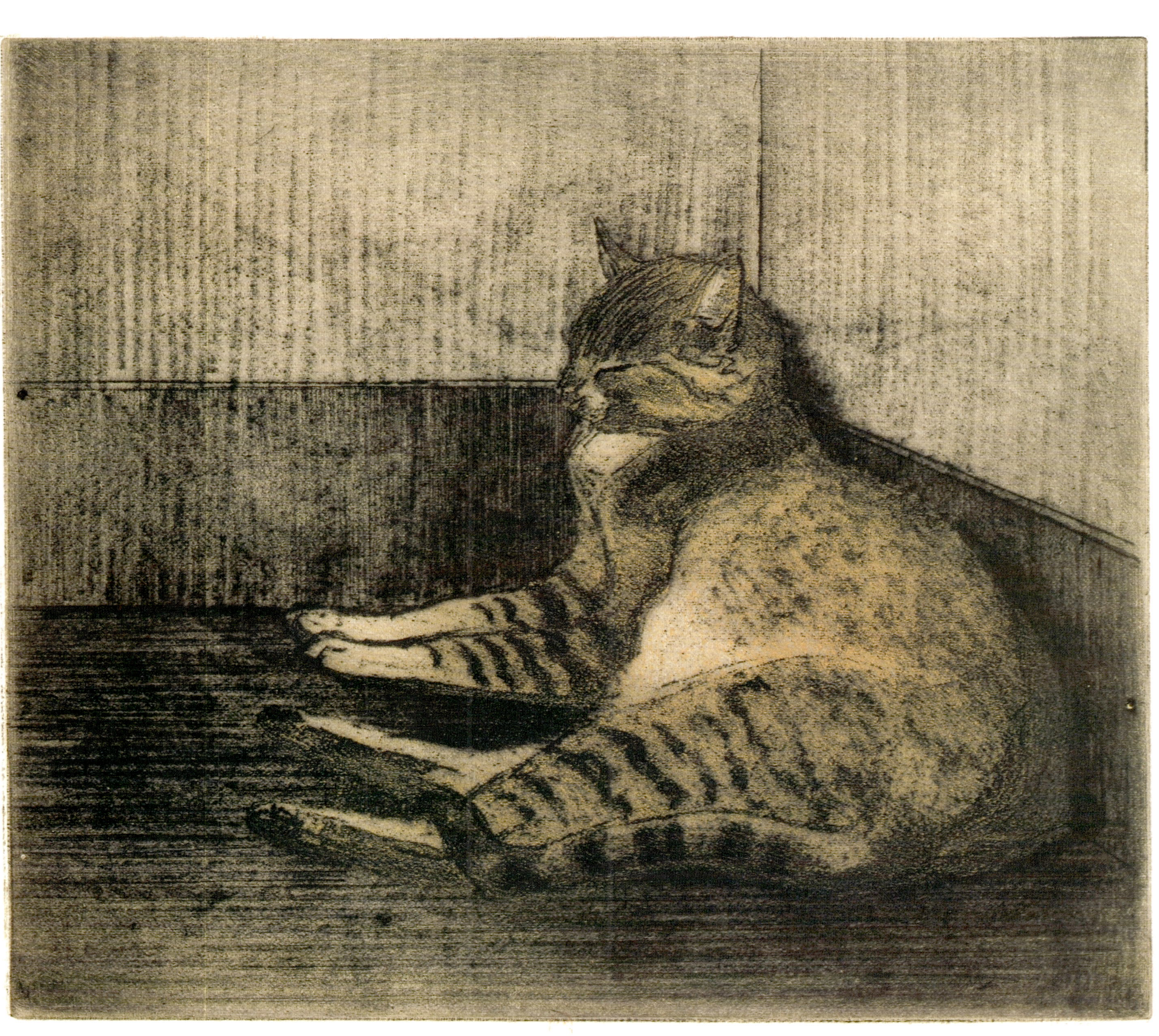

Plate 10

OLD CAT IN THE HAY

1902

Lying on its side in what looks like precarious equilibrium, this old cat is like an old fighter—its eyes blinded or perhaps just glazed with drowsiness, resting. Done a month after *Cat Dozing in a Corner* (Plate 9), this is another of Steinlen's prime cat studies from the peak years.

Soft-ground etching, aquatint, and
drypoint on zinc
7⅜ x 11⅝ inches (19 x 29 cm)
Second state of two

Crauzat 95

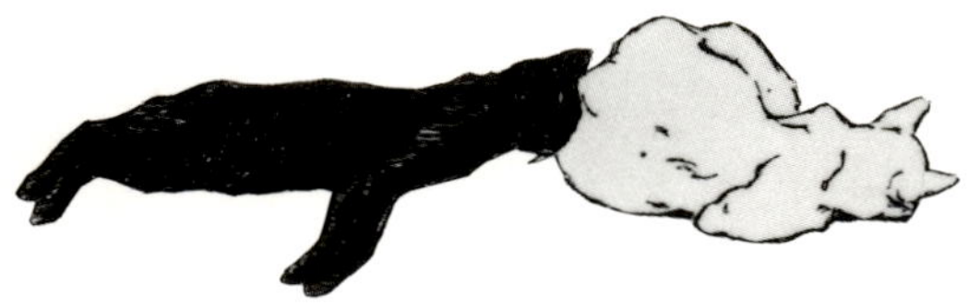

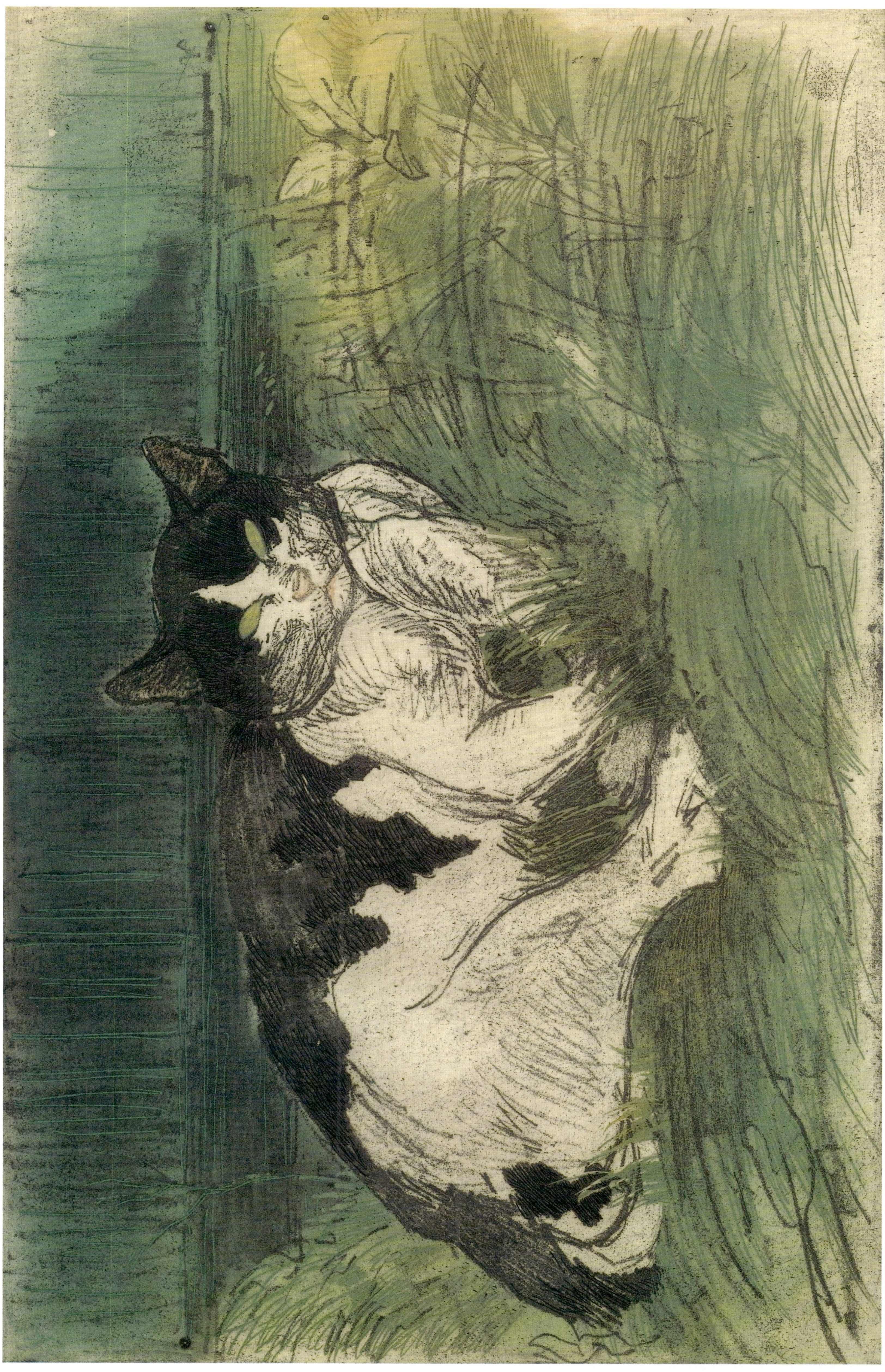

Plate 11

CAT LYING LEFT TO RIGHT

1902

The silky mottled fur invites caresses; with elegance and abandon, this short-haired cat lies stretched left to right, head resting on its paws in a perfect arc of a circle whose two points seek to join. Its book-ended twin (Fig. 9) lounges right to left. Together these two prints bring this masterful group to its climax.

Soft-ground etching, aquatint, and drypoint on zinc
4¾ x 9¼ inches (12 x 23 cm)
Single state

Crauzat 98

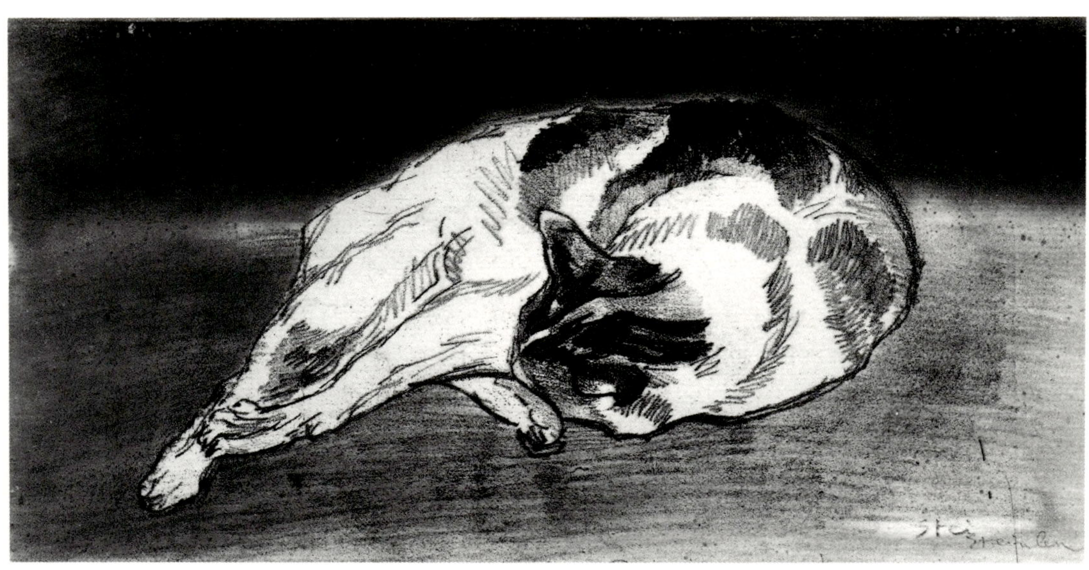

Fig. 9 *Cat Lying Right to Left.* 1902. Soft-ground etching and aquatint on zinc, 5⅕ x 10⅝ in. (13 x 27 cm). Crauzat 101

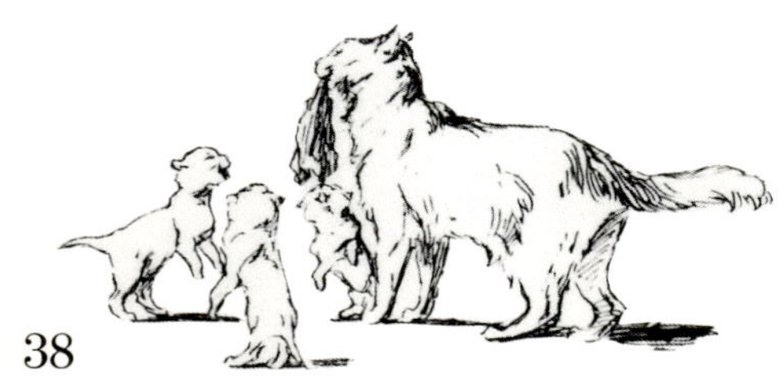

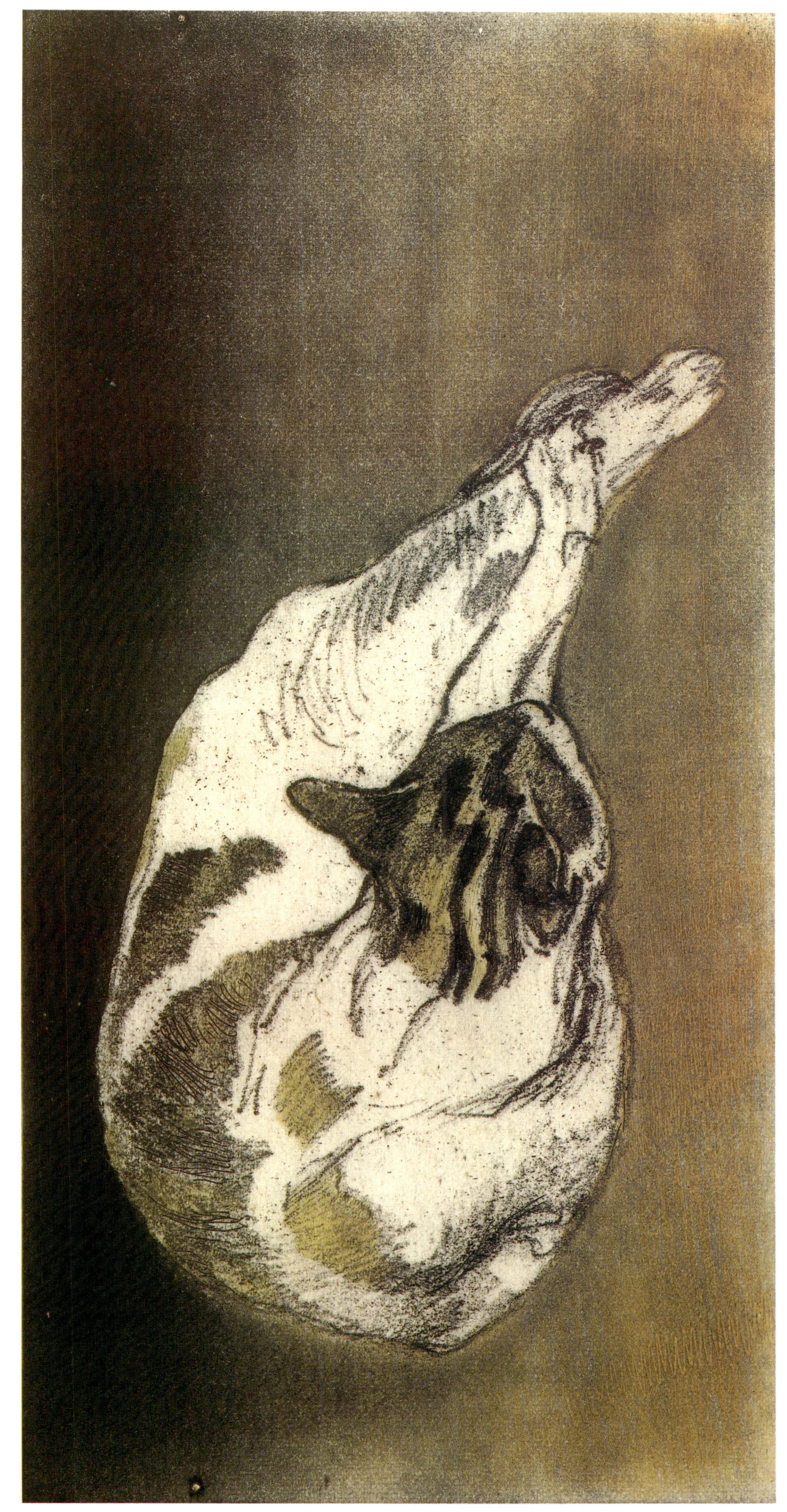

Plate 12

CAT WITH HEAD IN PROFILE

1903

Here is the white cat again, this time propped against a wall with its right paw tucked under its chest and its left one stretched out and over the right hind foot. This is a more complicated pose, but a less successful composition than those from the previous year (Plates 9, 10, and 11 and Figs. 9 and 10). Seen on this page, the latter was etched in the summer of 1902. This white cat also props itself against a wall, but plants its front legs wide apart. Steinlen brought the cat's back to the foreground and tucked in the composition with a simple and pretty curve of the tail. Above all, his fondness for these creatures is evident in this piece; it is a study of a cat, not merely an interesting object.

Soft-ground etching and aquatint on zinc
4¾ x 9¼ inches (12 x 23 cm)
Single state

Crauzat 103

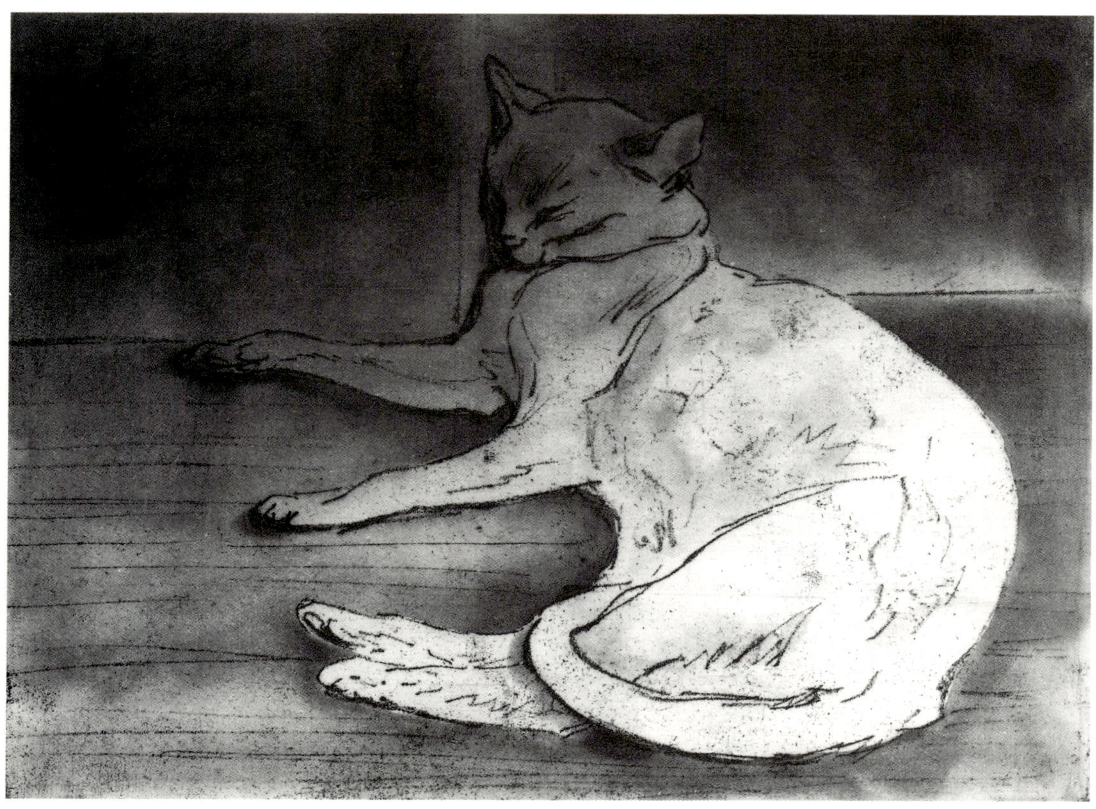

Fig. 10 *Cat Lying in the Sun.* 1902. Soft-ground etching and aquatint on zinc. 7 x 9¼ in. (18 x 23 cm). Crauzat 96

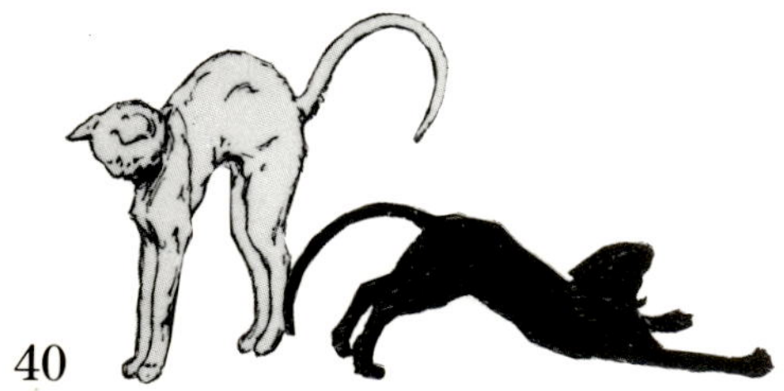

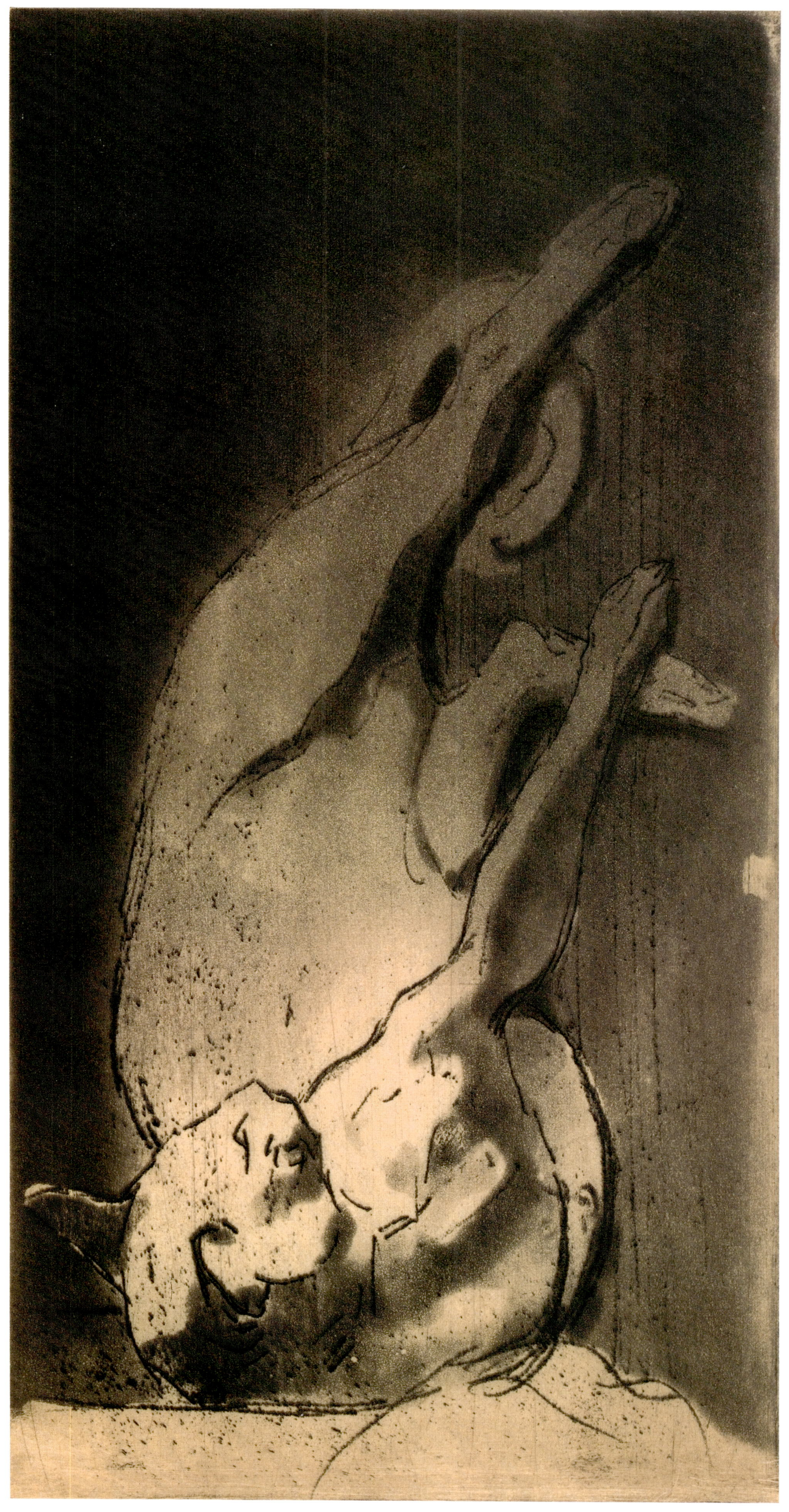

Plate 13

PUBLICATIONS OCTAVE BEAUCHAMP CALENDAR

1902

Colette, or a memory of her, reappears in this Art Nouveau-style calendar. She is still wearing her red dress, and she is still confronting a cat. The wicker chair from the back cover of *Des Chats* (Plate 6) is her fortification. Around the borders, Steinlen's cat furies have also made a comeback. The black angora has just leapt up to claim the new year, sending the tabby into mad flight with the old year. In rather incongruous contrast to the symmetrical, linear flourishes of the border and flowers, cats have taken possession of the calendarium below. The ash-gray cat poses like a sphinx above the border of September, just behind October's crouching tiger. They are flanked by a meowing pantherlike cat and a coiled black-and-white.

Drypoint etching on copper, type, and heliogravure
21¼ x 14¼ inches (54 x 36 cm)

Crauzat 35 (etching); Bargiel/Zagrodzki 80

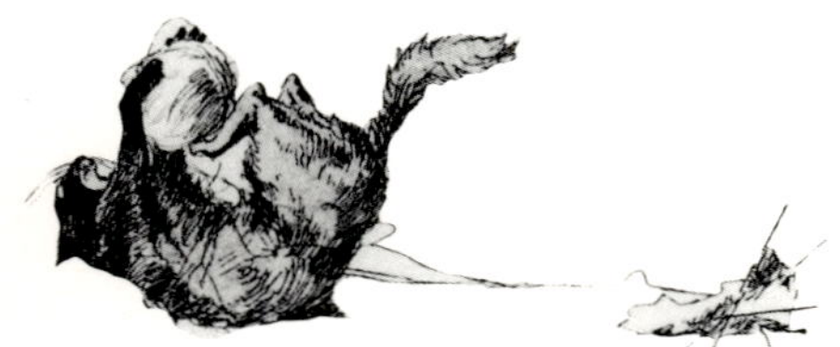

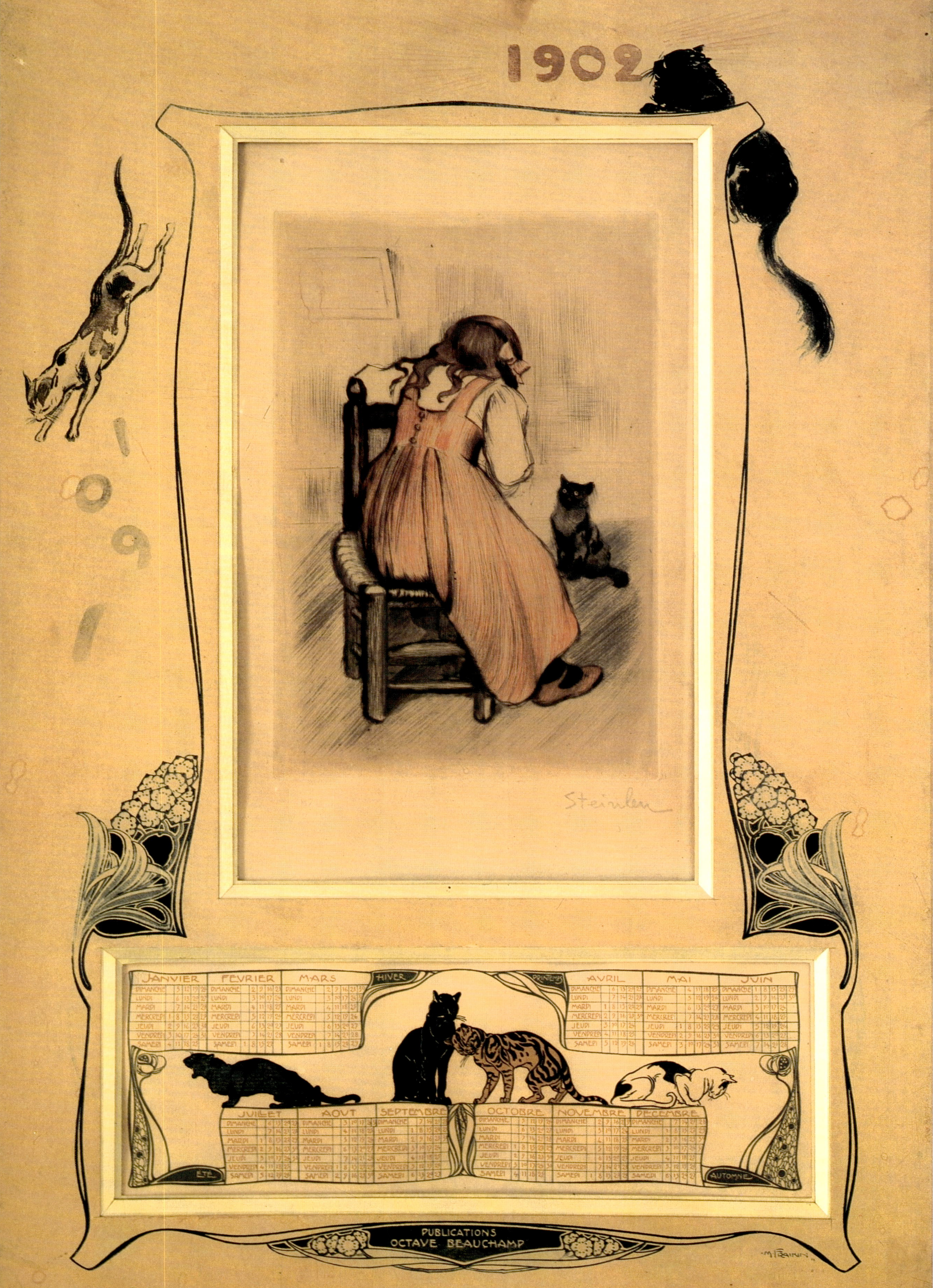
1902
1901
Steinlen
JANVIER
FEVRIER
MARS
HIVER
PRINTEMPS
AVRIL
MAI
JUIN
JUILLET
AOUT
SEPTEMBRE
OCTOBRE
NOVEMBRE
DECEMBRE
ETE
AUTOMNE
PUBLICATIONS
OCTAVE BEAUCHAMP

Plate 14

CLINIQUE CHÉRON

Chéron Clinic

1905

Once more Colette is back, but what a change! Fifteen years have passed since she posed for her father with the bowl of Vingeanne milk (front cover and Plate 1). Her signature red dress is printed with sprigs of white flowers and trimmed with lace; a fillet secures her familiar reddish-blond hair. There are still animals at her feet and, now, at her head.

The large poster advertises the most fashionable veterinary clinic in Paris: "Chéron Clinic, specialist in veterinary medicine, 8 rue de Moulins (at avenue de l'Opéra). Sanatorium. Boarding. Telephone 14106." The writer Colette mentions the clinic's proprietor, Henri Chéron, several times in her novels—a literary, if not commercial, endorsement of the clinic's standing. As always, the animals are wonderfully observed. A languid collie solicits a caress under the chin, a bulldog stands on hind legs against Colette's dress, while a brown hound fondly lifts a heavy muzzle toward her. In the upper part of the poster, four cats, having scaled the placard, vie with each other in demonstrating their affections: the black one with velvet paws purrs under her caress, the skinny black-and-white massages Colette with its talons as it leans into her cheek. Each creature in its own way begs for attention, enters a claim, hangs on, and waits: an animal comedy rendered with an accuracy and simplicity that overshadows the subject of the poster and even the figure of Colette. This great poster, executed with crayon, scraper, and spatter lithographic technique, is one of the last lyrical images; soon afterward, tenderness is abandoned in favor of harsher and more emotional themes.

Color lithographic poster
77½ x 55⅛ inches (197 x 140 cm)
Printer: Ch. Wall, Paris

Crauzat 511; Bargiel/Zagrodzki 45

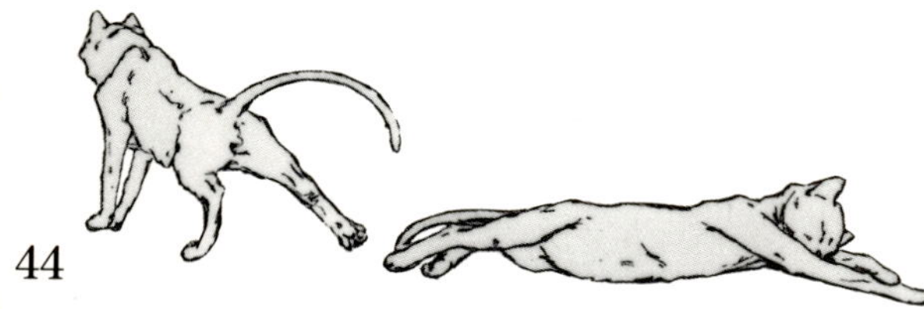

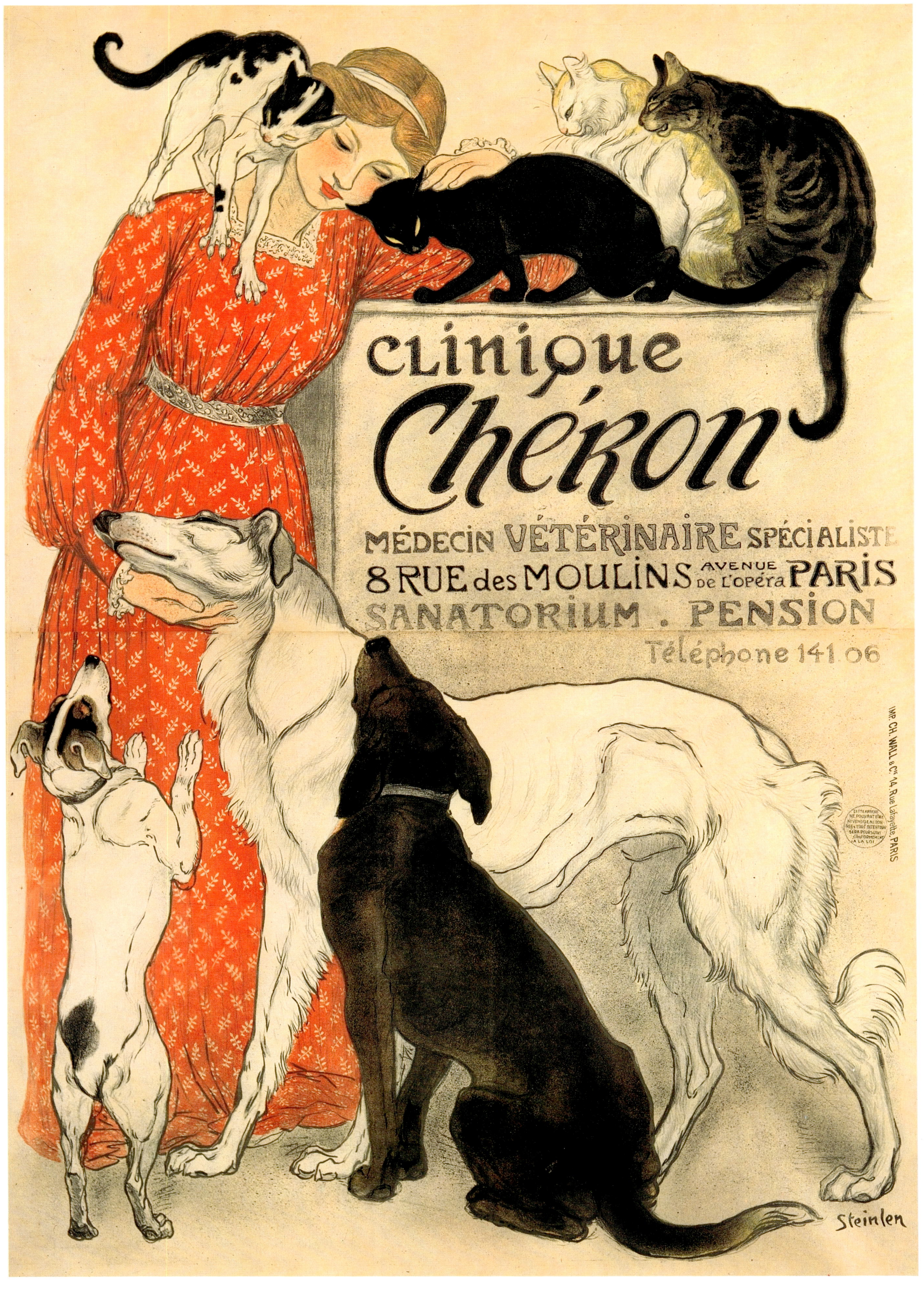
CLINIQUE
Chéron
MÉDECIN VÉTÉRINAIRE SPÉCIALISTE
8 RUE des MOULINS AVENUE de L'Opéra PARIS
SANATORIUM . PENSION
Téléphone 141.06
IMP. CH. WALL & Cie 14. Rue Lafayette, PARIS
CETTE AFFICHE NE POUVANT ÊTRE NI VENDUE NI DONNÉE, TOUT DÉTENTEUR SERA POURSUIVI CONFORMÉMENT A LA LOI
Steinlen

Plate 15

WINTER. CAT ON A CUSHION

1909

Half playful, half serious, the animal with the magnificently rendered winter fur is an enigmatic creature, the picture of distrust. It lounges on a red cushion, daring one to approach. But compared to the etched cats of 1902 (Plates 9, 10, and 11 and Figs. 9 and 10), this is a cat manqué. Although the lithographic technique gives the fur a sensual tactility, the drawing is less than convincing.

Steinlen used the same composition as the field for a poster, printed by G. Frichot, advertising the second exposition of animal artists of the Cercle International des Arts (Fig. 11).

Metropolitan Museum of Art. Gift of Henry J. Plantin, 1950

Lithograph
19½ x 23¼ inches (49 x 59 cm)
Printer: R. Engelmann, Paris

Cruzat 293

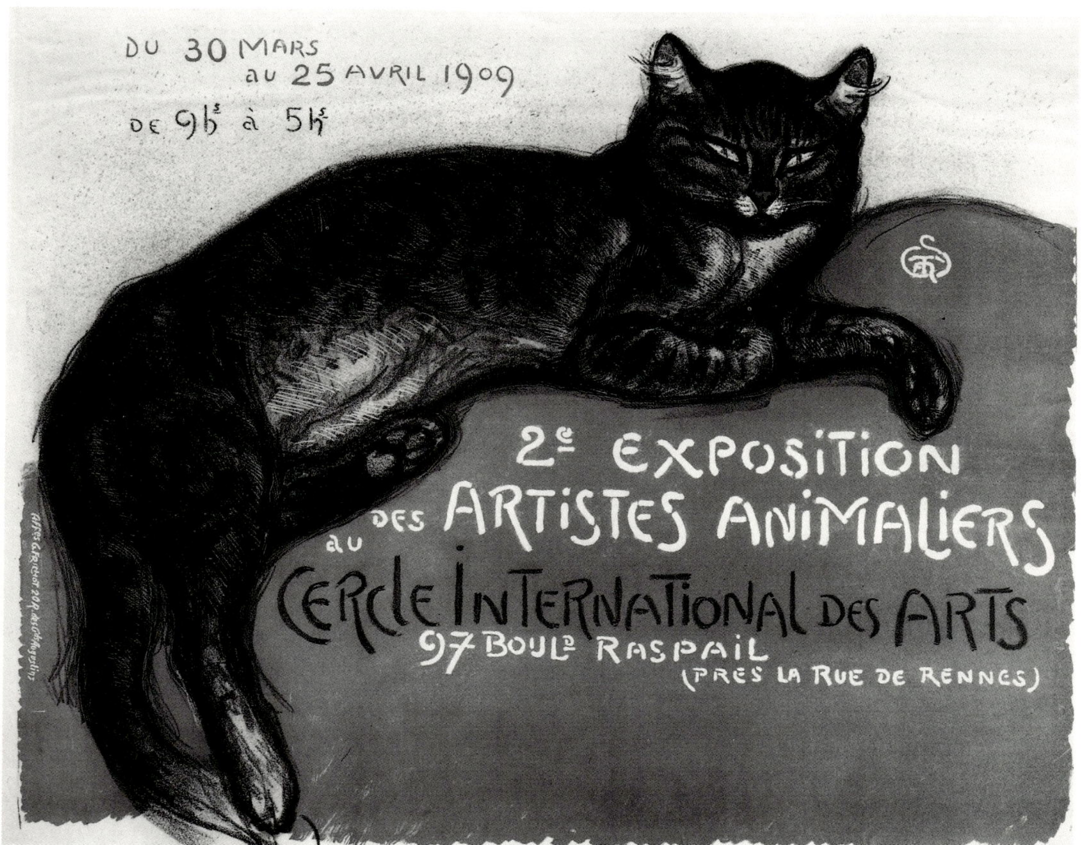

Fig. 11 *2e Exposition des artistes animaliers.* 1909. Lithographic poster, 19⅞ x 25⅜ in. (50 x 64 cm). Printer: Affiches G. Frichot, Paris. Crauzat 517; Bargiel/Zagrodzki 50

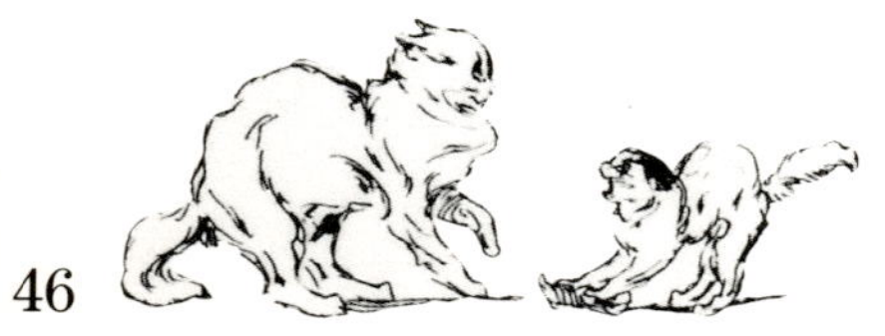

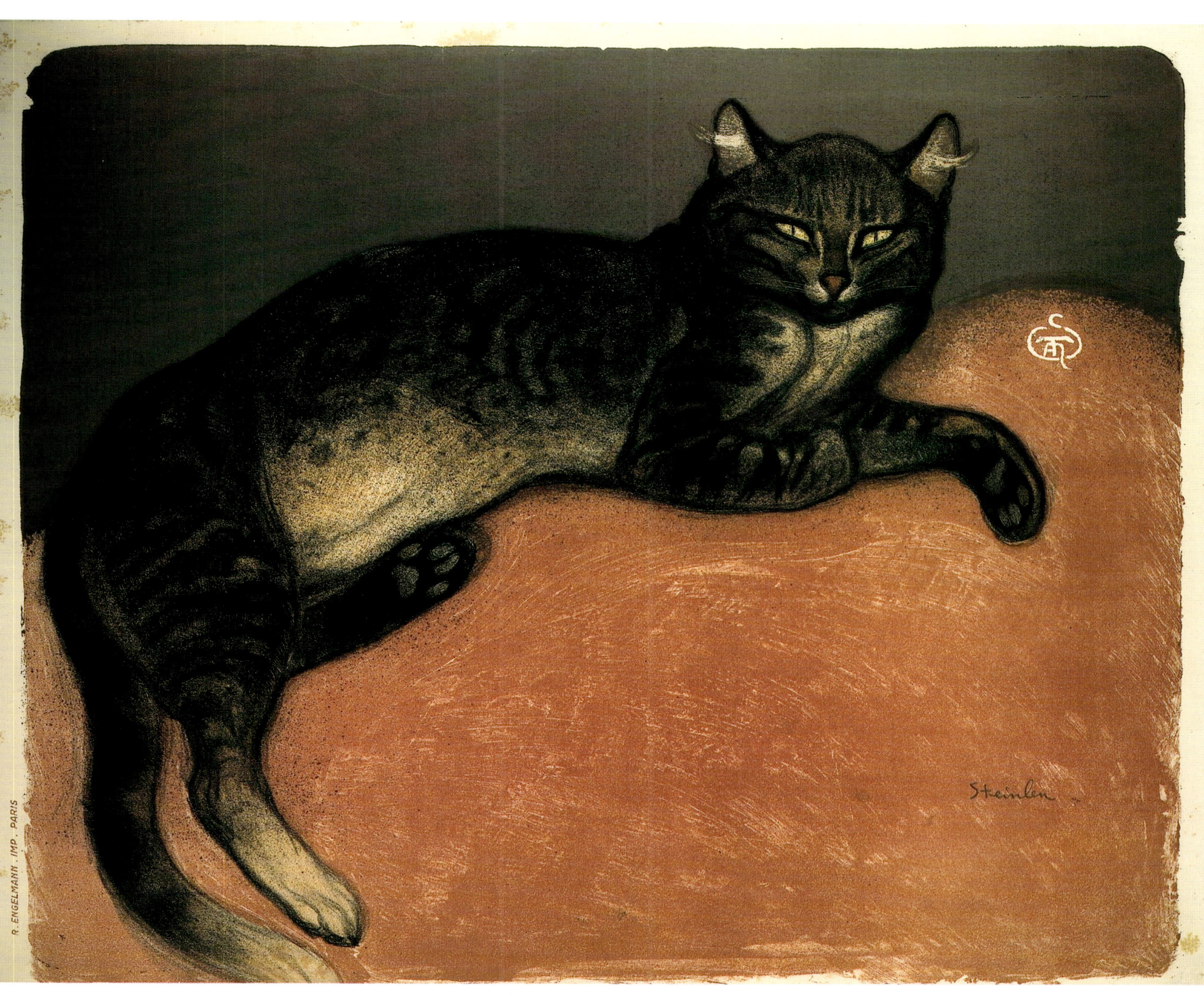
R. ENGELMANN. IMP. PARIS
Steinlen

Plate 16

SUMMER. CAT ON A BALUSTRADE

1909

The cheetahlike cat of summer drops a hind leg and its tail over the edge of the railing to catch a breeze. Its yellow eyes squint less with ferocity than with lassitude. This decorative print, made as a companion to and probably sold with *Summer* (Plate 15), fills the sheet better than its counterpart but shows some of the same improbabilities in the pose—the front legs, for example—as if Steinlen had drawn it from memory.

Lithograph
19½ x 23⅞ inches (49 x 61 cm)
Printer: R. Engelmann, Paris

Crauzat 292

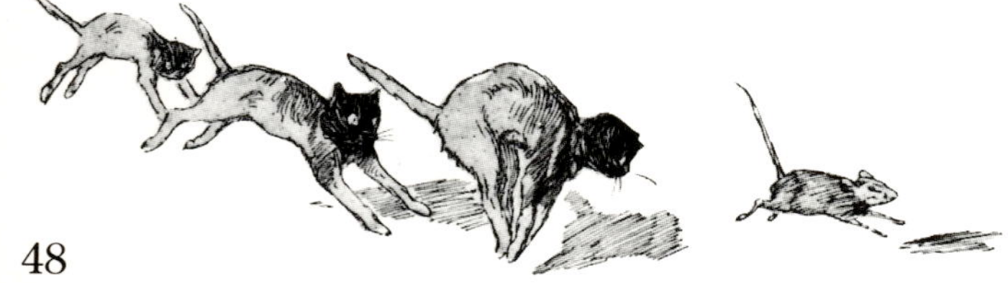

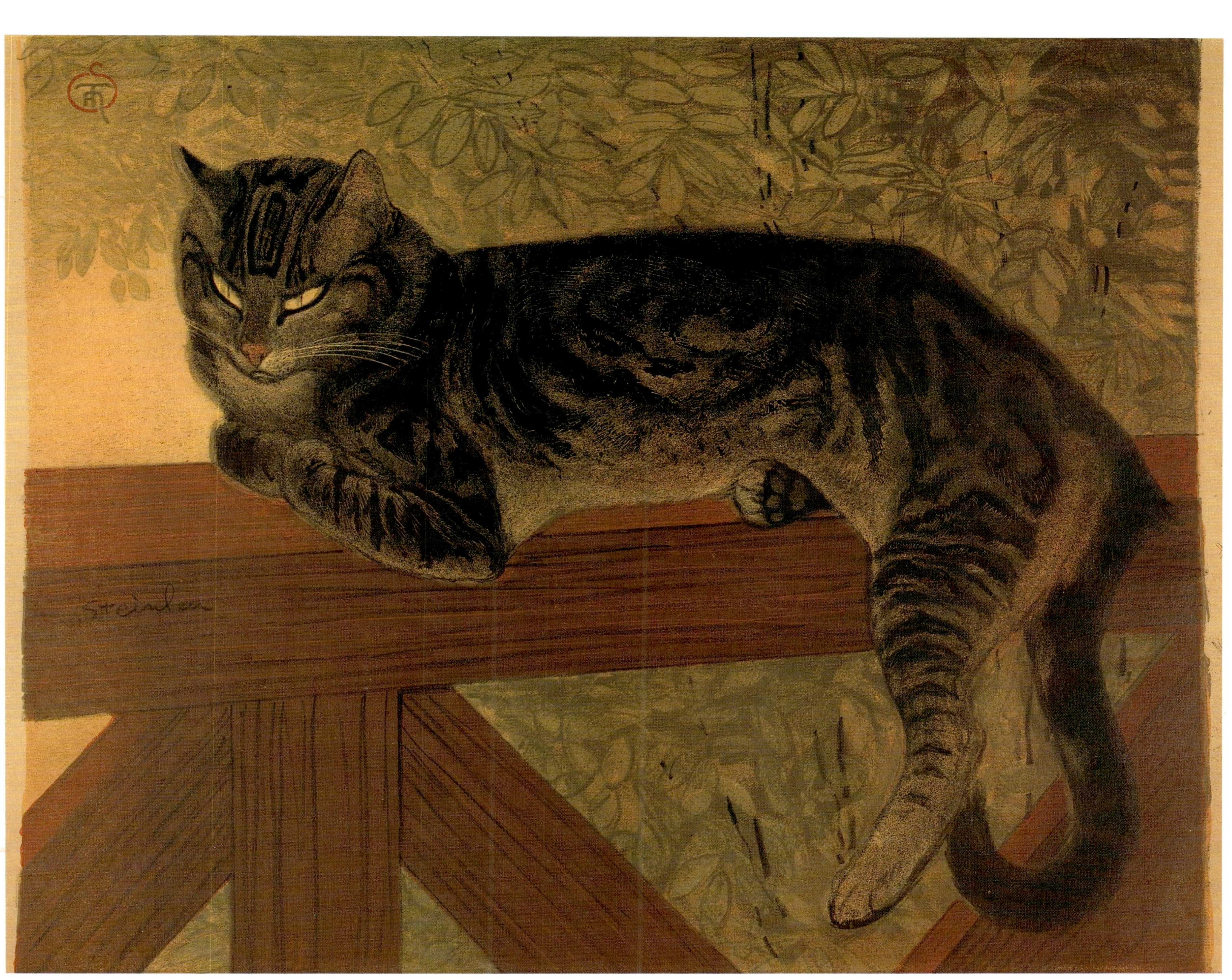
Steinlen

Plate 17

"LE LOCATAIRE"

The Tenant

1913

The tabby and little girl cling to each other, heightening the poignancy of this homeless family's plight. In fact, Steinlen composed the group to make the sad child and her pet the anchor of the picture. Made in 1913 to announce a new publication of a tenants' federation, this work shows clearly the direction Steinlen had taken as World War I came on. Images like this—which poured forth in every graphic medium—endeared Steinlen to his contemporaries.

Color lithographic poster
63 x 47 inches (160 x 119 cm)
Printer not given

Bargiel/Zagrodzki 53:A1

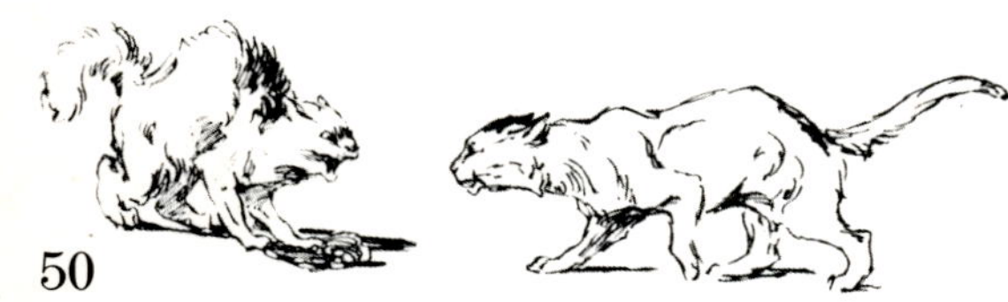

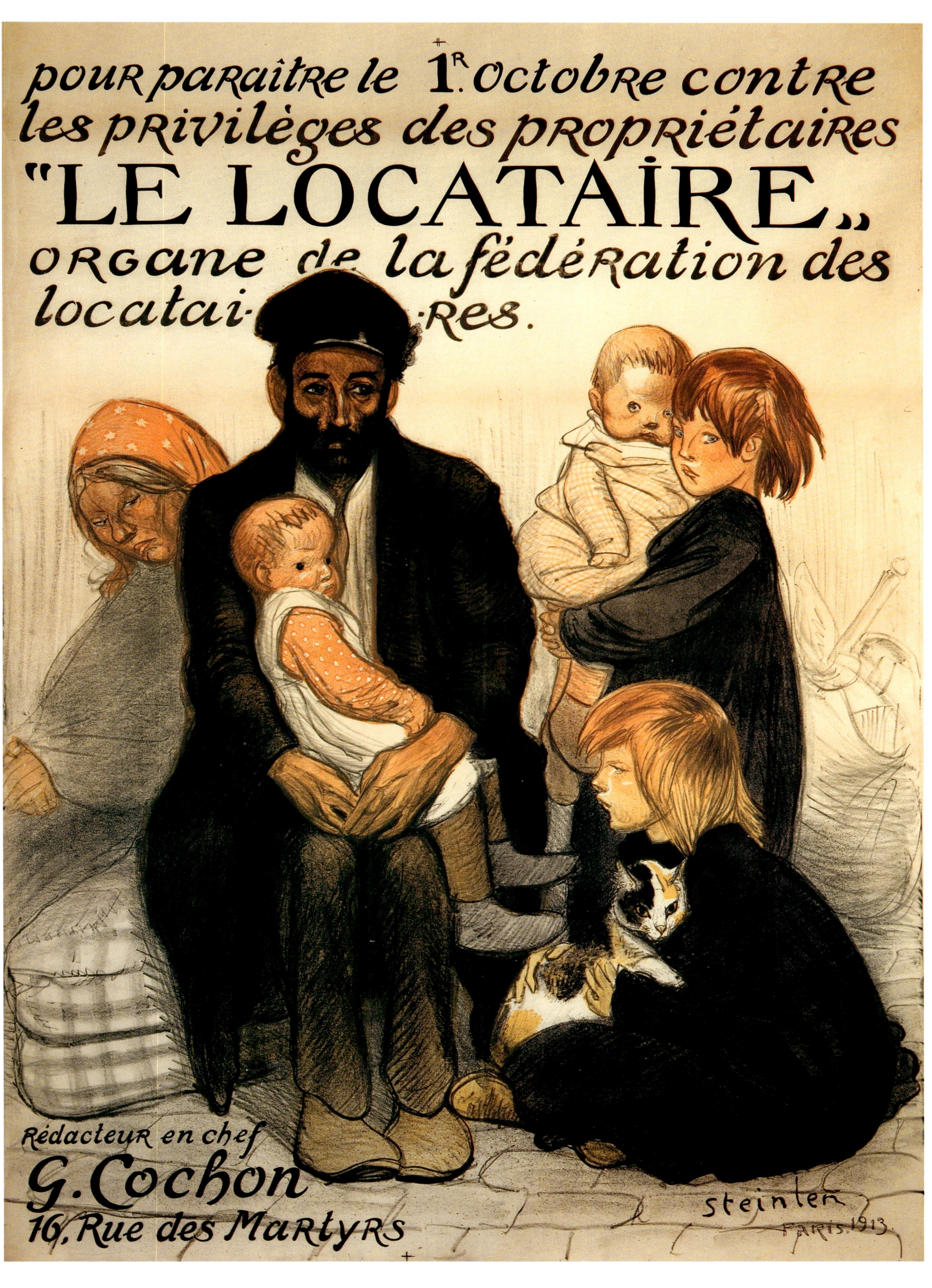
pour paraître le 1r. octobre contre
les privilèges des propriétaires
"LE LOCATAIRE"
organe de la fédération des
locatai- -res.
Rédacteur en chef
G. Cochon
16, Rue des Martyrs
steinlen
PARIS 1913

Plate 18

VIOLET CAT

Before 1901

Not signed and only attributed to Steinlen, the question is: Could anyone but Steinlen have created this magnificent creature? Printed larger than life, *Violet Cat* represents the apotheosis of catness, the cat in attainment of divine status. The blazing eye, tense throat, proud ruff, and trainlike tail are all achieved with the economy of form that only a master has the confidence to attempt. Timeless, this ranks with the great cat images of all time.

Lithograph
65¾ x 46¾ inches (167 x 119 cm)

Bargiel/Zagrodzki 77

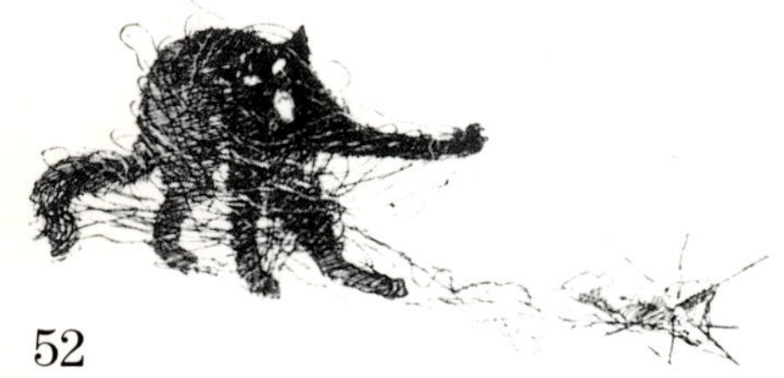

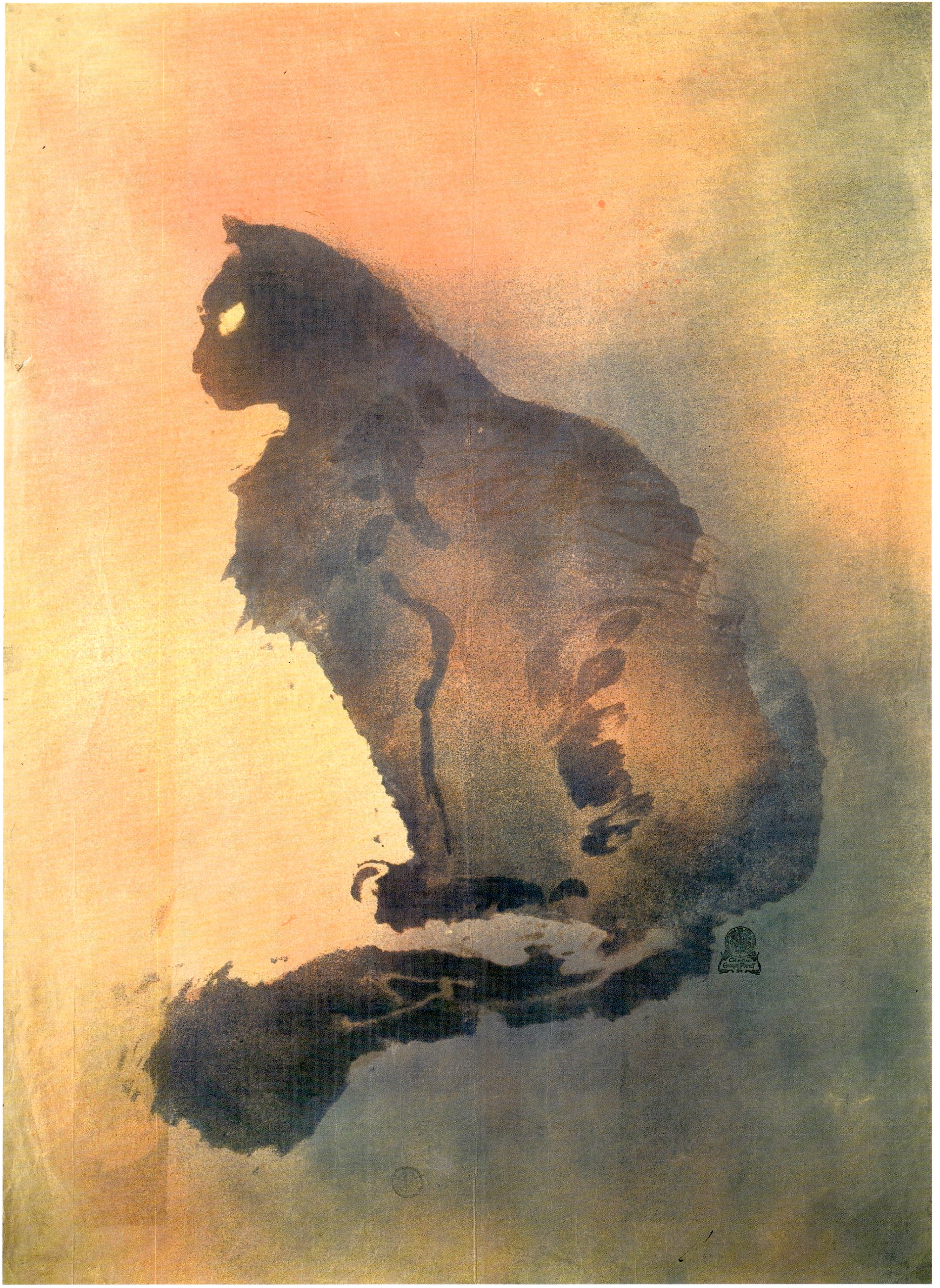
Collection
Georges Pochet

Plate 19
(Front cover)

COLETTE WITH BOWL OF MILK

1894

Several versions of the design for *Lait pur stérilisé de la Vingeanne* (Plate 1) were produced without lettering, including this superb oversize version. The strong, flat colors of Colette's dress and hair and the emphatically asymmetrical composition show Steinlen's internalization of two influences: Japanese prints and the aesthetic of Art Nouveau.

Lithograph
68⅛ x 59⅞ inches (173 x 152 cm)
Printer: Charles Verneau, Paris

Crauzat 491; Bargiel/Zagrodzki 16:B2

Plate 20
(Back cover)

À LA BODINIÈRE

La Bodinière Gallery Poster

1894

For their debut poster appearance, in this 1894 poster for an exhibition of his own drawings and paintings at Galerie La Bodinière, Steinlen's cats already are perfected creatures. The tabby, seen in three-quarter view from the rear, winks invitingly; the black cat, drawn in profile, is the essence of feline reserve. Both cats are familiar from the Vingeanne milk poster ensemble (Plate 1 and front cover). As if proof were needed, Steinlen's identification with cats is witnessed by his artistic monogram, seen in the upper-right corner of the poster, in which his initials are a calligraphic suggestion of a cat seen from the back.

Lithographic poster
24 x 32¾ inches (61 x 83 cm)
Printer: Charles Verneau, Paris

Crauzat 492; Bargiel/Zagrodzki 14:A6

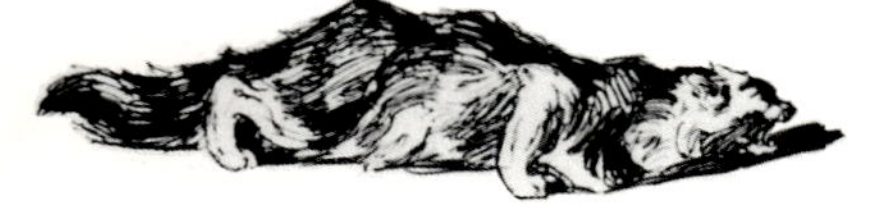

PRINCIPAL SOURCES

The following publications have served as the principal sources for the information contained herein:

Réjane Bargiel and Christophe Zagrodzki. *Steinlen affichiste: Catalogue raisonné.* Lausanne: Éditions du Grand-Pont, 1986.

Phillip Dennis Cate and Susan Gill. *Théophile-Alexandre Steinlen.* A Peregrine Smith Book. Salt Lake City, Utah: Gibbs M. Smith, 1982.

Ernest de Crauzat. *L'Oeuvre gravé et lithographié de Steinlen.* Paris: Société de Propogation des Livres d'Art, 1913. Facsimile edition published by Alan Wofsy Fine Arts, San Francisco, California, 1983.

Ebria Feinblatt and Bruce Davis. *Toulouse-Lautrec and His Contemporaries: Posters of the Belle Epoque from the Wagner Collection.* Exhibition catalogue, Los Angeles Museum of Art. New York: Harry N. Abrams, 1985.

Claude Roger-Marx. *Graphic Art of the 19th Century.* Tr. by E. M. Gwyer. New York: McGraw-Hill, 1962.

Théophile-Alexandre Steinlen 1859–1923. Exhibition catalogue. Berlin: Staatliche Kunsthalle, 1978.

All illustrations have been referenced in accordance with their listings in two *catalogues raisonné:* Bargiel/Zagrodzki (posters only) and Crauzat (complete work to 1913). Both are listed above.

Photo credits

Phot. Bibl. Nat., Paris, supplied all illustrations except as noted here:

Jean-Pierre Laubscher, Éditions du Grand-Pont, Lausanne: Figs. 1, 6; Plates 13, 18. Metropolitan Museum of Art. Gift of Henry J. Plantin, 1950: Plate 15. Jack Rennert, Posters Please, Inc., New York: front cover; Figs. 2, 3; Plates 1, 2, 14, 17. Christophe Zagrodzki, Musée de la Publicité, Paris: Fig. 7

The publisher gratefully acknowledges the assistance of Mr. Jack Rennert of Posters Please, Inc., New York, in connection with the illustration of this book.

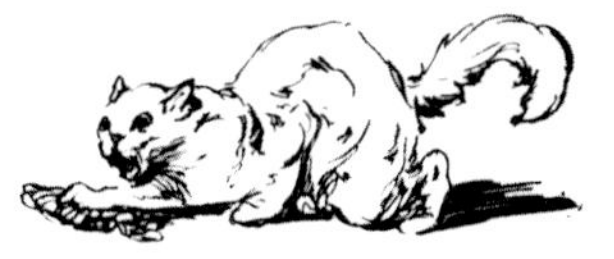

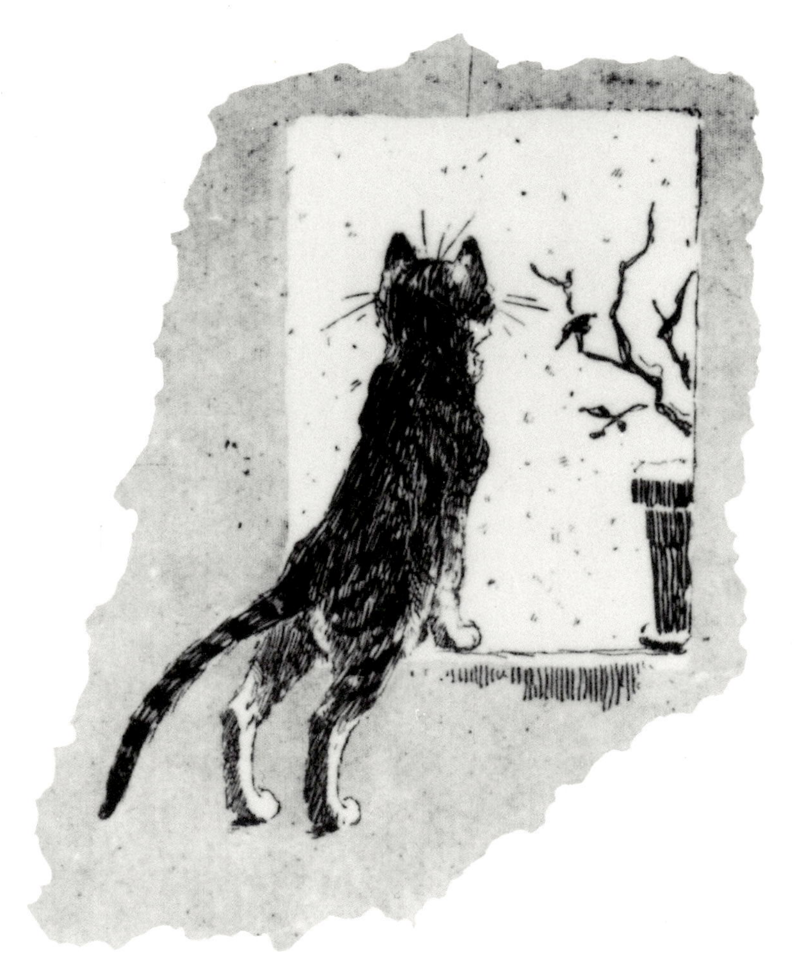